Interview

A Practical Guide to Be More Confident,
Overcome Anxiety While Giving Job Interview

(A Detailed Guide on How to Answer Interview
Questions)

Paul Dalton

Published by Rob Miles

Paul Dalton

All Rights Reserved

Interview: A Practical Guide to Be More Confident, Overcome Anxiety While Giving Job Interview (A Detailed Guide on How to Answer Interview Questions)

ISBN 978-1-989990-65-0

All rights reserved. No part of this guide may be reproduced in any form without permission in writing from the publisher except in the case of brief quotations embodied in critical articles or reviews.

Legal & Disclaimer

The information contained in this book is not designed to replace or take the place of any form of medicine or professional medical advice. The information in this book has been provided for educational and entertainment purposes only.

The information contained in this book has been compiled from sources deemed reliable, and it is accurate to the best of the Author's knowledge; however, the Author cannot guarantee its accuracy and validity and cannot be held liable for any errors or omissions. Changes are periodically made to this book. You must consult your doctor or get professional medical advice before using any of the suggested remedies, techniques, or information in this book.

Upon using the information contained in this book, you agree to hold harmless the Author from and against any damages, costs, and expenses, including any legal fees potentially resulting from the application of any of the information provided by this guide. This disclaimer applies to any damages or injury caused by the use and application, whether directly or indirectly, of any advice or information presented, whether for breach of contract, tort, negligence, personal injury, criminal intent, or under any other cause of action.

You agree to accept all risks of using the information presented inside this book. You need to consult a professional medical practitioner in order to ensure you are both able and healthy enough to participate in this program.

Table of Contents

INTRODUCTION 1

CHAPTER 1: OPENING QUESTIONS 2

CHAPTER 2: THE INTERVIEW PROCESS............................. 11

CHAPTER 3: DRESS TO IMPRESS 17

CHAPTER 4: COMPANY RESEARCH.................................... 23

CHAPTER 5: EXPERIENCE RELATED QUESTIONS 37

CHAPTER 6: WHAT YOU DO & DON'T WANT IN A CAREER CHOICE 56

CHAPTER 7: HOW IMPORTANT IS IT TO LOOK GOOD IN AN INTERVIEW? 63

CHAPTER 8: PRESENTATION - DISCOVERY 67

CHAPTER 9: HOW TO FILL OUT APPLICATION FORMS CORRECTLY.. 72

CHAPTER 10: PRE-INTERVIEW PREPARATION: DETAILS OF YOUR STORY 77

CHAPTER 11: THE PERFECT ATTIRE 91

CHAPTER 12: GIVE YOUR INTERVIEW THE RIGHT CLOSING 105

CHAPTER 13: GETTING INTO INTERVIEW STATE............. 108

CHAPTER 14: TOP JOB INTERVIEW QUESTIONS 112

CHAPTER 15: STEPS TO TAKE AFTER YOUR INTERVIEW.. 129

CHAPTER 16: PREPARE FOR THE INTERVIEW 132

CHAPTER 17: SALARY NEGOTIATION 136

CHAPTER 18: BEGIN THE INTERVIEW 145

CHAPTER 19: FINDING JOBS AND NETWORKING 154

CHAPTER 20: MOST COMMON INTERVIEW MISTAKES .. 168

CHAPTER 21: WRITING A GREAT RESUME 178

CHAPTER 22: WHAT ROLE DO YOU TAKE IN GROUP PROJECTS? 184

CHAPTER 23: QUESTIONS AND ANSWERS: THE TOP 50 TOUGHEST QUESTIONS 188

CONCLUSION... 194

Introduction

This book contains proven steps and strategies on how to do great in job interviews.

Interviews are usually the most dreaded part of the application process. It is perceived by the companies, on the other hand, as the most efficient means to assess prospective employees.

This book tells you the secrets on how to ace any interview. You will be briefed on how to prepare for the interview, how to maintain your calmness, how to answer specific questions, how to dress, and what things you should avoid. This compendium is written in a very simple manner and the tips are very practical. Hopefully, this will be instrumental for you to get the best life ahead.

Thanks again for downloading this book, I hope you enjoy it!

Chapter 1: Opening Questions

Tell me a little bit about yourself.

This, without a doubt, will be one of the first questions asked when it comes time for your interview. Even if there was a part of the application process that asked you this, you will still be likely to have to answer in person. They want to hear first and foremost about who you are. This is their opportunity to get to know you. Here, they want to get a sense of how you feel about yourself. Many positions will require confidence and self-assurance. You'll want to let them know that you are self-aware and that you believe in yourself and your own abilities.

To answer this, start off with what you believe is most important about yourself. Follow up with a brief history of your experiences, and then discuss why you are here at the interview and why you are looking to land this position. This may make for a short answer, but it is a good outline for what you will want your answer to be as well. Remember to recite your answer out loud or else it might end up sounding awkward when you really try to discuss who you are and your past achievements. This is an example of what you might say:

I began my professional career first as a mail sorter. From there, I managed to work my way up into various human resource positions. I eventually decided to go back to school to get my degree in communications, and now I'm looking to even further my career!

What are your strengths and weaknesses?

These interview twins always come together. Interviewers may ask for your biggest strength and weakness, may ask you to list three of each or may leave the type of answer up to you. Although talking about yourself without seeming boastful can be difficult, most people can usually come up with a list of strengths. These are the things you are good at that are also related to the job. An employer looking for a sales clerk is probably not going to be interested in your ability to put furniture together without the instruction manual. Instead, they are looking for outgoing, innovative and creative communicators. Think about what skills will be required to do the job and what matching skills you have. Have them ready before the interview in anticipation of this question.

When it comes to weaknesses, many people struggle. No one is perfect and you should always list at least one weakness.

At the same time, you should not provide a litany of things you cannot do. Come up with a few areas you know you can improve and provide those as weaknesses. Some good answers include, I have a hard time letting my boss know I'm too busy, I struggle with delegating work, or I would like to improve my understanding of database security. You can tie that last one in to anything related to the job. Employers are not looking for robots. They are looking for skilled people who can learn and grow with the job.

Why do you want to work here?

You can assume your interviewer realizes you probably need a paying job, a good insurance plan and a stable work environment. Avoid launching into the epic tale of your job search and how you really need a paycheck. Instead, talk about why you want to work for that particular company. If the company makes kid's clothing, tie in a love of children and fashion. If you are applying for a management spot, talk about how you have enjoyed bringing a team together to meet goals since you played high school sports. For an administrative assistant job, provide some of your organizational traits and talk about how you love to help creative and business geniuses thrive by taking care of the little things.

What about this position makes you want to work here? Why do you want to get hired?

The Why do you want to work here question is always going to be in the interview. It's not a trick question! Your interviewer will legitimately want to know why it is that you chose them. The obvious answer is, Because I need a job and I saw you were hiring. I want money. This is usually the first thing that we will consider when applying to a job. While this might be the truth, try to honestly remember why it is that you want this position and not another. Have your reason prepared before even making your way into the interview. When you can give substantial answers based directly on their mission statement, then that will give you a big advantage.

I want to work here because I have always been a lifelong supporter of this company. I have frequented the stores and I understand what the clientele is like. Not only do I think this will help me to be more passionate and dedicated to my work, but I think it helps because I will be more knowledgeable about what the business actually stands for. When I have this connection to the workplace, it is easier to go above and beyond because I have the confidence to know what my talents are and how the company will benefit from them.

How did you find out about this current position?

The reason that employers might want to know this is because it will reveal even more about you. First, they are going to want to know if you know anyone that already works there. This gives them a personal recommendation which can be helpful in understanding who you are. They are also going to want to know if you were actively job-hunting and being proactive about finding a new position, or if this is just something that slipped into your lap. They are also going to be interested in figuring out if any of their marketing tactics to reach out to other potential candidates are working or not.

I actually found a listing for this job on an online job board. I have been looking and applying to several places and the objectives and job description of this position intrigued me.

Why did you apply for this job?

Don't say that you've applied for the job because of better salary or benefits; rather, say that you applied for the job because its job description is a perfect fit for you and that the company's vision-mission and goals are in line with your own.

What do you know about our company?

This is where your research efforts truly pay off. Mention the most recent news about the company that you know. Be sure to mention good news about the company. Highlight its awards or achievements. By mentioning these, it makes sense as to why you got interested to apply for a position to the company. In addition, mention the company's current goals and concerns, to which you can respond or help by offering your skills and expertise.

What separates you from other candidates?

Answer this question by emphasizing your strengths. Don't say anything bad about other candidates. You don't know them anyway, but you know yourself so focus on mentioning your pleasant and unique capabilities.

Why should I hire you?

This is your chance to show your confidence about the job. The key to nailing this question is by being observant of the interviewer's expectations and preferences for the ideal candidate of the job. Generally good answers to this question include stating that you should be hired not only based on your qualifications and experience, but also because of the fact that you will be a valuable asset to their organization and that you can be expected to perform well in the offered job.

How do you see yourself in five years?

A lot can happen in five years, and this question tries to assess the degree of ambition and realism, which you have in you. A good answer can sound something like, in five years, I see myself promoted to the position of area supervisor, managing and mentoring my own team, and having contributed significantly to the company, starting with a sales increase of at least 100% of the account assigned to me.

How do you find our office?

This question examines how observant you are, and how quick you can assess your immediate environment. You want to answer this question by stating the positive characteristics of its office. For instance, you may say that their office is spacious and professional-looking so that it offers an ideal work environment that's good for business.

Chapter 2: The Interview Process

The first step in landing any job knows your qualifications. If you want to be a Rocket Scientist, it would be best to know and understand what qualifications will be required. One way to do this is by looking at job postings for the job you are chasing and comparing your personal resume with what is being asked. For the sake of this book we will assume you have all of the qualifications for the position and we will move on to the interview process.

Every candidate will need a concise resume and cover letter written specifically for the position for which they are applying. Ensure with every cover letter the specific company and exact position title are addressed and even if your qualifications exceed a one page resume, it is best to try and keep your credentials to no longer than two pages. The best would be one page. Often, overly large and elaborate resumes will deter potential employers as the human resources department will often vet through the applications prior looking for ones which are not well written, poorly organized or overly lengthy.

If you are able, having an online resume to expand on your shorter, more concise application, will aid those who have furthered interest in your capabilities to view your longer and more detailed credentials. Including your personal mission statement and any keywords often used to describe the position, within your resume and cover letter is another helpful way to show the hiring committee you share the same values. Often, hiring committees will weed out applications, which do not include these items.

Now that your resume and cover letter are primed and set for success, you are onto the next step, which is going through the interview process. Each company will conduct their interviews in a slightly different manner but there will always be key elements which remain the same.

Weather your interview is over the phone or in person you may be required to interview for the position more than once.

It is also important to remember that every interview process will be a little different because every company and every interviewer is different. Every interviewer has their own perspective and ideas which they feel are most important for the position they are hiring. If the person conducting the interview is the person who will also be your boss they may have their own ideas about how their team will best function which will ultimately lead to different types of questions and different types of details they would like from you.

It is important to prepare for a variety of questions and variations of those questions so you are capable of answering each question quickly with efficiency and attention to detail. It could also be that the interviewer will simply use text book questions and not attempt to customize the interview process.

Depending on the industry for which you are applying questions can be more technical, behavioral, or even specific to the job or field of work. While it is difficult to say exactly how an interview will be performed we can do our best to break down the basics of the interview process and give you a good idea of what to expect. Do your best to impress your interviewer and convince them of your fit with the company within the first five minutes. Studies have shown that interviewers make up their mind about a candidate within the first five minutes and the rest of the interview is just confirmation about their decision. Those first five minutes are crucial. Come into the room with high energy and enthusiasm and make sure to tell them how appreciative you are of the interview. Remember that you may not be the only person interviewed that day and depending on what number in line you are, the interviewer may be tired and feel as though they have been playing a broken record with the same answers the entire day. You want them to remember you. Start out with a positive comment such as "I have really been looking forward to this interview and meeting you. I think your company is doing great work and I am excited by the idea of becoming part of the team."

Interviewers often view interviews as adversarial. It can seem as though candidates are trying to pry a job offer out of the interviewer. The interviewer's job is to hold on to that offer until they are convinced by the interviewees pitch for the job. You need to transform the tug of war dynamic into a relationship where you are on the same side as your interviewer.

Begin by opening with kind words about the company and stating how happy you are to learn more about the company from someone who currently works there and provide some background information about yourself so you can figure out if this will be a good fit. Stating that you always think it is unfortunate to hire someone who turns out to not be a good match making no one happy will gain you some points with the interviewer for sure.

Chapter 3: Dress To Impress

When you go to a job interview you are dressing to impress your future boss. You may spend money investing in a new business suit that you are hoping you will soon be wearing to your new job. Even with the best suit you can sometimes encounter pitfalls that even the most experienced job seekers can fall into. You could fail your job interview and not know why if you are not aware of these pitfalls that may arise.

If for example you have sweaty hands and you are not even aware of this because you have your mind on preparing for your interview. As soon as you shake hands with your future boss with a cold sweaty hand, he is going to translate that into you being a person that lacks self-confidence, not the kind of person he wants on his team. Right then and there you have lost your chance at this job. Let's face it most people are not too fond of getting a wet and sticky hand shake. This is something that does not make a good first impression.

You may feel that a wet hand, or a wrinkled shirt, and uncombed hair are very trivial things. You believe that your superb skill set and solid background is enough to ensure that you will be hired. The problem is if the future employer doesn't like your attitude that comes out in the sloppy way you present yourself, they are not going to hire you, they will go with someone else.

It can be very hard at times for interviewers to decide on what candidate to hire. Sometimes they will resort to basic tactics by eliminating the candidate who looked tired. If for example you had to work a long shift before your interview it may be worth your while to mention to your interviewer that is why you look so tired during the interview. You may get the job because your future employer is fair and reasonable and was understanding of your situation. If you do not explain why you look tired they may go with someone else.

Importance of First Impression

Many experts have stressed that the first impression is very crucial when trying to make a good impression to others such as future boss. The best way for you to give a good impression to your future boss it to make sure that you are dressed well and groomed for the interview.

Dressing appropriately at your interview is important because not only will your future boss be deciding if he wants to hire you, but future teammates will be giving you the once over. Future teammates will be deciding if you are someone they will want to work with. These decisions will be based on your appearance during your interview. The teammates will be spending one third of their life with you so there is no way that they will pick up someone they do not like.

The truth is once you are at the point of being chosen for an interview, the other candidates will have similar skill sets making not much difference between you. Therefor when it comes to small things like your personal appearance this is going to have a critical effect on your future employee deciding whether to hire you or not. It may boil down to something as simple as they liked the color choice of tie you wore to the interview. Perhaps your tie had their company logo colors in it.

Don't Have to Spend a Small Fortune

Don't think that in order to make a good impression during an interview that you must go out and spend a small fortune on clothing, and a new hairstyle and cut. It is not necessary that you add to your credit card bill at a time when you should be watching your spending especially if you are out of work. You do not want to go overboard where you end up looking like a person that does not belong on the team of the future boss that you are trying to impress.

If for example you are a lady you do not want to apply at a financial institution wearing a sheer low-cut blouse, mini skirt and big high heels, looking more like a fashion sexy model. You want to try and blend into the crowd that you will be working beside, you will have a much better chance of getting the job if you look like you will fit in with their team.

Perfume during an interview

You love to wear perfume it is great at showing off your personality, style, and taste. Who isn't wearing perfume, and who doesn't love perfume.

When it comes to a job interview you must be very careful with your perfume during a job interview. Make sure that you wear only a small amount. Remember that you are going to be in an enclosed room for at least forty minutes. If you are wearing strong perfume this may put your future boss off, it may cause them to feel poorly.

The worse thing that could happen is that your future boss is allergic to the type of perfume that you are wearing. If this happens then you can be sure that your interview is going to be over in a flash.

You don't want to wear the same perfume that your boss's ex used to wear, you could be out the door because your choice of perfume brought forth bad memories for your boss.

Go with a Subtle Nice Smell

It is very important that you smell nice and fresh when going into your interview, while at the same time you are not overwhelming your boss with strong perfume.

A lady should wear only a bit of scented lotion or perfume. Don't put the perfume on just before your interview this will make it smell too strong.

A man should use a very light touch of cologne or aftershave.

Make sure that your breath is fresh when you walk into your interview. Do not chew gum or be sucking on mints during the interview.

Chapter 4: Company Research

Your resume is pretty telling about the skills, experience, and qualifications that you hold, then why do companies hold such extensive and oftentimes excruciatingly nerve-wracking interviews? They do so to understand if you are a good fit for the company. Whether or not you will follow their vision, adopt their mission, and adjust well into the company. By researching the company, you immediately get an edge over your interviewers. By understanding the company's vision, their environment, and culture, you can phrase your answers to echo the same vision. Fortunately, in the current Digital Age, it is not very difficult to research companies. Almost every business has an online presence today. Your understanding of your prospective employers is just a Google search away.

The Website

This is the first place you need to visit. The company's website will have outlined everything you could possibly need to know about them. But don't just read about their background or map out the location, be thorough with your research. It will give you valuable information that you can use during your interview. Primarily, you should check the About Us section to read up about the history and the current practices of the company. The About Us section is a good place to know the background, mission, and goals of a company. Doing so would better help you understand the company's operations and values. Also, scour through the rest of the website to look for important keywords that will be indicative of what the company is actually looking for and the culture. For instance, if they use words like 'we are a family of...' then know that the culture is very friendly and warm. You can phrase your interview answers to resonate the same values that is, if you truly believe in them.

Social Media

Social media is a good place to check how the company wants to be portrayed to its prospective customers. How do they engage with them? What types of information do they share with them? All this information can really help shape your answers. Check all popular platforms of social media, including Facebook, Google+, Twitter, and Instagram. What platforms are they most activate at? What medium do they use most to communicate? Do they share motivational content, information only, visuals? Companies that don't have an active social media presence or NO presence probably have a more traditional approach and might value the same from their candidates.

LinkedIn

LinkedIn is a really good place to learn more about the company. Company profiles on LinkedIn have a plethora of information available. You can check for news on jobs posted recently, promotions, connections and company statistics. All this is valuable information that can be greatly assistive in understanding the company's operations. How many jobs have the company posted recently? Does it show that they are scaling? How long has the position you have been applying for been open? If it has been open for too long, it could mean they are pretty selective or perhaps are not offering great value for the position. Also, if you see connections, you could reach out to them to know more about the company and get some inside scoop. They may even be able to put in a good word for you. You may also want to check out your interviewer's profile on LinkedIn. This will help you get an insight into their position and background. Also, look for connections or links between the two of you. Did you go to the same college? Have the same interests? Know the same people? Are part of the same groups or circles? All this information can help establish great conversation points during the interview. However, don't be too obvious about your research. You don't want to shake hands and tell them how you follow the same groups on LinkedIn. That will sound a bit intrusive and borderline creepy.

Glassdoor

Glassdoor is an amazing portal to get some inside scoop on the company. You can get tons of important information from the platform regarding the company's operations, the employee's opinions, and even other important information like salary figures, company reviews, and employee duties and functions. You may also find information related to the hiring process like details about the questions that will likely be asked, who will most likely be interviewing etc. Know that since all the information is based on personal experiences, it may not always be violets and rainbows. Often times, employees with grievances lash out their frustration on Glassdoor, and it may not always be reflective of the company as a whole. You want to look for patterns. Is there a common problem with the management or salaries that a lot of the employees are facing? If yes, then it most likely is a serious problem and one you should consider before applying.

Products, Services, and Clients

Say you are applying to a digital marketing company. You probably would have some idea about the services they offer. But you need to focus on what aspects do they truly excel in, who are their clients and how do they communicate with them. A good place to look for this information are white papers, case studies, and Google search.

Find a Connection

Ever heard of the phrase 'It's not what you know, but who you know?' Not to say, having a connection is a sure-fire way to land a job, but it sure can help with the process. Hiring managers would consider someone that has been recommended to them. Recommendations are a great way to let your skills and talents do the talking and make the case rather than a single interview. There are plenty of ways to find a connection. Good thing we live in times when finding a connection is a few clicks away. A simple search on your social media platforms will help you find a connection to a company. For instance, just go to the company's page on Facebook. How many of your friends have 'liked' the company? Check those friends profiles and go through their About sections. Are they currently or previously have worked for the company? If yes, then send them a Direct Message requesting some information. You can then go on to ask if they'd be willing to slip in a recommendation. You can also reach out to close friends, family, and even previous co-workers asking if they know someone in the company. A little word-of-mouth can go a long way in helping you score your desired job. You don't even have to wait for a job opening to do this. If you have a specific place in mind that you'd love to work at, just get the word out. Let anyone who would listen know that you really want to work at the company. It could be at your gym, yoga class, alumni from your university, waiting area for the parents at school and even the guy behind the counter at your local coffee shop. You never know who would know someone who could help a friend out, but the first step is to reach out. The idea is to stay in the loop. Be active on your career-related groups on social media. Those are one of the places companies reach out to before going to news portals with job openings.

Most companies would spread the word before they make a job posting, and having the word around that you are looking for work, you immediately will become the first person that pops into a person's mind when a job vacancy opens up. Say, you let the manager at the nonprofit organization you volunteer at know that you are looking for work in the finance department. One of his connections reaches out via his social media portal that the company is looking for an accountant; the manager tags you in the post and messages you that he has shared a word about you and the manager is expecting a message from you. You contact the manager, he looks at your CV, and makes an appointment for the interview.

By just getting the word out, you not only managed to find a job posting, but applied for it with little to no competition. Now you can just move on to the next leg and ace that interview.

Key Players

Don't just dig up information on the interviewer; you want to have some background on the key players in the company too. You can use this information to answer questions regarding inspirations and goals. Understanding the key player's journey through the company would be helpful in understanding the skills and experience required to make a powerful impact on the company. Sure, it sounds a bit too ambitious, but it is the ambition that gets you places!

Any Recent Events and News

Search for the company on Google. What all comes up? Is there any note-worthy information out there that you, as a prospective employee, need to really know about. Any mergers, downscaling, expansions, controversies that can help shape your answers better? Also, check Google News to read up on the latest scoop regarding the company. Knowledge of the recent events of the company and slipping them in through the interview will be a good indicator of your interest in the company. It will show that you have indeed prepared for the interview and are desirous of working for the company.

Company Culture

This is one of the core reasons you go through such a lengthy interviewing process, to begin with. Companies don't want to hire someone that would compromise on the culture. The culture of a company is extremely important in establishing a healthy and productive workflow. The companies know about it, and they don't want anyone compromising with it. Some companies like Zappo even conduct culture-fit interviews just to check if a prospect would fit into the company's vision and culture. They want someone that would adapt and embody that culture like their own. Be that person. A good way is to reach out to someone you know in the company to talk to you about the culture and employee relationships. Is the culture laid back and respectful? Is it about motivation and values? Understanding the culture can help set the tone for the interview, and you will be able to structure answers that resonate with the company's voice.

Know Their Competitors

You need to know about the market that you are working in. Who are the company's greatest competitors? Many times, hiring managers do bring this question, but you need to be prepared with the information at your arsenal. The objective of this information is not on how to tackle the competition but rather to know whether or not an applicant is aware of the industry, their products and services, and their market position in general.

Inside Scoop

This is where all the juicy bits come in. Don't go probing too much or too obviously. But if you have found a connection, then it could really help to get a better understanding of why the job is up for grabs, how the previous employee was, why did he leave or was fired. All this information will help you determine what the company is actually looking for and how to present yourself as the best option for the same.

Your Interviewer

In most cases, you will be told about who will be interviewing you. They may tell you a name or the designation, but beyond that, you could either depend on guesswork, or a little research. There may be just one person taking the interview or perhaps a team. Ask the Human Resources of the company for the names, titles, and roles of the interviewers when they call/e-mail you to set up an interview. Hiring managers usually have an HR person contact the candidate in person to determine whether or not they are truly interested in the position offered and whether they are suitable to move forward. This screening interview is oftentimes conducted via a phone call or Skype.

This is also a good time to ask them about the hiring process, how many interviews and screenings do they do before the final verdict. Also, ask about who would be taking and attending each interview. HR recruiters are usually very accommodating about providing these details. All this information will help you map out the process and prepare accordingly.

Company research is an essential component of the overall job interview since it shows respect for the people that you desire to work with and to let them know that you have indeed done your homework. Even if you lack in skills and experience, your preparation and determination will more than make up for it. The recruiters will sure give preference to someone really wanting to learn and work with them than someone with a fancy resume but no drive.

Chapter 5: Experience Related Questions

What would your boss say is an area you could improve on?

Question Type:

Background and Personality

Question Analysis:

The interviewer will use this question to assess how well the candidate embraces critical feedback. No matter how strong a performance review might be, most managers will offer up at least one area for improvement. The interviewer is looking for the candidate to be candid about an area for improvement and discuss how they are taking action. Ideally, your response would discuss an area you are new to and investing time to improve.

What to Avoid:

You should avoid criticizing your boss's judgement. A response such as "my boss told me I need to pay better attention to detail but I disagree with her assessment" will not go over well with the interviewer. It will portray you as someone who is not receptive to critical feedback from superiors. You should also avoid saying something such as "my boss has never suggested an area for improvement." Remember that this question is a hypothetical. If your boss has not provided critical feedback, then you can still come up with your own area for self-improvement. Finally, you should avoid discussing areas that would be concerning to the interviewer. If you are interviewing for a sales position and you mention that you need to become better at communicating with customers, you will create a cause for concern.

Example Response:

My boss would say I could get better at recognizing when my work load is at full capacity and delegating work. I recently moved into a supervisor role, but I still put too much on my own plate which causes me unnecessary stress. When tasks and projects come up I tend to gravitate toward taking full ownership over them instead of working with my team to find out who is in the best position to do the work.

I recently implemented weekly update meetings with my team so that we can run through everyone's workload and availability. These meetings have helped me identify opportunities to delegate project work throughout our team to create a better balance for everyone.

Why is there a gap in your employment history? (if applicable)

Question Type:

Background and Personality

Question Analysis:

If the interviewer asks this question they are looking for an upfront and honest response. The best way to approach this question largely depends on the reason for the gap. If you were laid off, you should provide some details of the situation and discuss why the company decided to reduce headcount. If you took a leave of absence, you can explain the situation from a high level but there is no need to go into too many personal details. For example, "I had a health scare I needed to resolve" or "a family member became ill and needed my full attention" is enough detail. You should try to incorporate positive items in your employment history before and after the gap. It is also beneficial if you can discuss your ambitious intentions during the gap period.

What to Avoid:

You should avoid getting defensive with your response. Your answer should not be centered around any excuses with past employment. Whether it was a result of a prior job or a personal reason that resulted in the gap, you should avoid going into too many unnecessary details.

Example Response:

When I previously worked at XYZ Company, they unexpectedly lost their largest customer and needed to take drastic action to stay in business. 25% of the sales force was laid off including most members on my team. It felt like a punch in the gut, but I understood the Company did not have much of a choice.

As I considered my next steps, I decided that it was important not to jump at the first opportunity but instead take the time to find the right fit for my career. I treated the job search like a full-time position, spending most of my days making new connections and setting up coffee or lunch meetings with business contacts in the area. I also made time to take a two-week online sales training course I had been interested in for over a year. After 4 months of networking and consideration, I decided to accept a position for a territory sales manager at XYZ Company.

What are three skills all professionals in this field should possess?

Question Type:

Industry and Company Specific

Question Analysis:

The interviewer will likely ask this question using the name of the profession such as "What are three skills all accountants should possess?" You should be prepared to discuss skills that are highly relevant to your profession and align closely with the job description. The interviewer is typically looking for the candidate to hone in on certain skill sets that are a must for the profession (i.e. excellent verbal communication skills for a nurse). The following skills are highly relevant to nearly all professions: Effective communicator, attention to detail, excellent planner, and strong time management.

What to Avoid:

Your answer should avoid overly generic skills that are presumed for all professionals such as "hard worker." Your answer should also not be a laundry list of skills. Be sure to discuss how each skill benefits the professional in their respective field.

Example Response:

(Example response is for accountants)

Successful accountants focus on attention to detail to ensure their work is complete and accurate. We work in a profession where small mistakes can have profound consequences. Attention to detail in this profession means fully understanding the scope of the work and expectations before completing it. It also means critical self-reviews before finalizing our work.

Accountants should also be excellent at planning their work at a micro and macro level. Time management is essential to staying on track and meeting deadlines.

Finally, all successful accountants should be effective communicators. Whether it is meeting with a boss, collaborating with team members, or discussing an issue with a client, accountants need to have strong written and verbal communication skills.

What was something you did not like about your previous (or current) position?

Question Type:

Background and Personality

Question Analysis:

This can be a tricky question because candidates are often tempted to heavily criticize their previous job or employer, but this can reflect poorly on the candidate's own personality and professionalism. You should discuss why you did not prefer a certain management style, a team dynamic, or a job limitation from a professional perspective.

What to Avoid:

Unless something drastic happened (such as fraud or harassment), it is important to stay away from character attacks or interoffice drama because the interviewer may associate it with your own personality. It is also wise to avoid criticism of common challenges that occur in most work environments such as "too much stress," "long hours," or "a demanding boss." These answers may lead to the interviewer questioning whether the candidate can handle adversity which will come up often in most positions.

Example Response:

Overall, I was really satisfied with my previous position. I worked with a great team and grew as a professional. I do wish I would have had more leadership opportunities in my previous role. The company was traditional in the sense that most project work was initiated and micro managed by the company's leadership. I thrive in an environment that offers leadership opportunities for all employees.

Question Type:

Behavioral

Question Analysis:

The interviewer will use this question to assess the candidate's team working capabilities. They want to know that the candidate possesses sufficient emotional intelligence to successfully adapt to the various personalities of co-workers. You should discuss an example that shows your ability to effectively communicate with a differing personality to achieve the desired results.

What to Avoid:

You should avoid criticizing a team member's personality. You should also avoid examples of working around another team member or excluding them from the work. The interviewer wants to see that you are able to adapt to various situations to find positive ways to work together with other team members.

Example Response:

S/T: Last year I lead a system implementation project with four other team members. I scheduled weekly update meetings to discuss the status of the project and to encourage collaboration on technical issues we were encountering. I noticed that one of our team members was extremely quiet during our team meetings, but he would often email me afterwards with excellent insight and ideas about the issues we had just discussed in the team setting. Not hearing his ideas until after our meetings was hurting our team collaboration. It was also inefficient for me to communicate his ideas back to the team versus all of us discussing them during the meetings.

A: I looked into his experience and employment history and noted that he had just graduated from college and joined the company one month prior. Instead of talking with him about the issue during the next team meeting, I decided to schedule a one-on-one meeting. I explained to him that I was a bit nervous and shy when I first started with the company and that it was completely normal. I also tried to boost his confidence by explaining how valuable his follow up ideas had been toward the project. I explained the benefits of speaking up during team meetings but made sure not to make him feel too much pressure.

R: Over the course of the next few weeks we all started to observe him grow more comfortable with sharing his input during the team meetings. While he may be disposed to a more reserved personality, the ability to acknowledge that and work with him enabled us to use his talents to add more value to our team.

Do you prefer working in a team setting or independently?

Question Type:

Background and Personality

Question Analysis:

This question can be tricky to some candidates because it sounds as if the interviewer is asking them to take up a definitive preference for one setting over the other. However, most positions require candidates to work both independently and within a group. Unless the job description explicitly calls for working independently or in a team setting at all times, the best response is to explain that you are comfortable working in both environments.

What to Avoid:

It is okay if you prefer working independently over working with a team or vice versa but you should avoid making a bold preference in your answer. The interviewer may view your strong preference as a sign that you are weak in the other area.

Example Response:

It largely depends on the situation. Some projects and tasks are best accomplished through team work and collaboration while others are more effectively completed through independent work. I have a do-whatever-it-takes mindset and feel comfortable as a team player collaborating in a group setting but can also buckle down and work independently when needed.

Did you get along with your prior boss?

Question Type:

Background and Personality

Question Analysis:

The interviewer will use this question to get a better sense of the candidate's ability to work well with superiors. The interviewer wants to know whether you create or burn bridges. You will usually only hurt yourself by heavily criticizing your previous or current boss. Unless your boss did something highly unethical or illegal, you should focus on a positive answer.

What to Avoid:

You should avoid personal insults and character attacks when describing your previous boss. If your answer is strongly critical of your boss, the interviewer will likely view you as someone who does not respect superiors or get along well with co-workers.

Example Response:

I enjoyed working for my former boss. She never let her team get bored with their work. I was always presented with new challenges and learning opportunities. She also placed a strong emphasis on team communication and had an open-door policy for new ideas. Her management style helped me grow as a professional.

What type of salary are you seeking?

Question Type:

Background and Personality

Question Analysis:

Unlike question #69, you should not offer up a dollar amount in your response to this question. Instead, focus your answer on your enthusiasm for the position and desire to receive a competitive offer. Effective salary negotiators typically avoid being the first one to throw out a figure.

What to Avoid:

You should avoid discussing a specific desired salary figure in your response.

Example Response:

I am excited about the opportunities that come with this position but have not focused on a specific salary figure. If you were to offer me the job, I would hope to get an offer that is competitive with the salary range for this position while taking into consideration my experience and skillset.

Tell me about a time you had to deal with a difficult co-worker. What was the outcome?

Question Type:

Behavioral

Question Analysis:

The interviewer will ask this question to assess the candidate's ability to manage conflict in the work setting. They want to know that the candidate will not ignite a conflict but will also not run away from it. Your answer should demonstrate that you are able to work through a disagreement in a professional manner and find resolution toward a common goal.

What to Avoid:

When discussing why a co-worker was difficult to work with you should avoid insulting them or getting into too many personal details about their character. Your answer should focus more on the resolution than the individual. You should also avoid discussing tedious or irrelevant conflicts such as "she always eats my lunch from the refrigerator."

Example Response:

S/T: In my prior role as a financial analyst, I was tasked with testing our key financial reports when updates were made to our ERP system. After a significant update, I noted that one of our accounts receivable reports was broken. The data it produced was critical to our quarterly reporting package which was due in three days. The systems analyst who managed the technical side of the financial reports was not responsive to my emails or phone calls and when I stopped by his desk to let him know the importance of fixing the report, he blew me off.

A: I was frustrated with his response and lack of interest in helping our team get the report fixed. However, I remained calm and requested a meeting with him to sit down for fifteen minutes to help clear the air. He apologized for not being attentive to our request and explained that he had five different projects going on and was working thirteen-hour days to keep up. We both decided it was best to schedule a meeting with him and his manager to explain our team's urgent situation and help prioritize his time.

R: After meeting with his manager, she was able to shuffle around some of his project work to ensure our report was fixed on time. They were both appreciative that I took the time to sit down with them to explain the situation and find a solution that worked well for everyone.

Chapter 6: What You Do & Don't Want In A Career Choice

You can narrow down your list in finding a suitable career by asking yourself some questions on what you do and don't want in a career. To claim what you do want in a career try and make a list of the things that you want to be part of your dream job. Then make a list of all the things that you do not want as part of your dream job. By writing these specifics down it will give you a much clearer image of what you are looking for in regards to a career choice. When you have to put it down in writing it will gather all the precise things that will build that perfect dream job for you. This exercise will help you to dig deep into your thoughts and really bring your ideas forth on the outline for your perfect dream job. By putting things in writing it makes them seem more real and attainable. You can go through this list each day to help remind yourself of things you will have to do in order to obtain this dream job or career. By visually seeing the things that you would like to achieve within your career will give you some incentive to work at reaching your goals.

You will need to work on a plan of action discovering the best way for you to go in order to obtain your dream career. Remind yourself of what it really is you want out of your career that would make it a dream job. You will have to make some serious choices such as possibly making a total change in careers in order for you to get that dream job that you want to be part of your reality.

Now we all know that we can't always get what we want but by using the chart from chapter 2 will give you a list of your 5 main values to build on to develop a career you can be happy with. You must remember when choosing a career there may be things in a job that are not perfect but are they something you would be able to work with?

If there were things that you have the ability to improve would you be willing to do this? You may have to build on your career job in order to make it the perfect dream job. Perhaps you should consider a job with a company that is one that will encourage you to express your creative ideas. It may be important to try and find a job with a company that you feel is going to encourage you to expand and grow within the company. When you list what your dos and don'ts are in a career choice it really helps you to zero in or narrow your search window for that perfect dream job or career that you are seeking. By deciding what the most important factors to a dream job are to you will help you in finding more clear pathways towards reaching your end goal. Getting rid of the stuff that is standing in your way to heading in the right direction. This could mean getting rid of things such as bad habits such as drinking too much alcohol. This will be a bad distraction for you alcohol abuse will lead you away from your dream job not closer to it. Being able to stay focused and put your skills to use in accomplishing things along the road towards your dream job means that you must be willing to make some sacrifices in your lifestyle to enable you to obtain your goal.

Preparing for an Interview

When going for an interview you want to make the best first impression with your potential future employer. You want to make sure to say the right things during your interview not the wrong things. Below are a few examples of things you should not say during an interview followed by a list of things you should say.

Do Not Say:

1) "How long before I can be eligible for vacation?"

2) "How much vacation time will I get?"

3) "How long before I accrue additional weeks of vacation?"

By opening your interview with these kinds of questions you are going to sound like someone who can't wait to finish work before you have even been hired. It is important that you ask questions during your interview but not about taking time off. Even if you are more than qualified for the position you are interviewing for you can still make the wrong impression by asking the wrong question at the interview. You certainly do not want to show up late for your interview this could make the prospective employer think if you are late for your interview how often are you going to be late once and if you are hired. Make sure to turn your cell phone off before your interview. If your phone rings do not ask the interviewer if they mind if you take the call. That would be disrespectful of them and down right rude, better yet just leave your cell phone at home or in your car.

When you are asked what your weaknesses are don't say you are a workaholic this will not impress the interviewer but show them that you are unwilling to admit to your weaknesses. The interviewer knows that all candidates have weaknesses if you are honest and admit to yours they will respect this. Instead of discussing skills that you will gain by getting the job try and point out what skills you will be bringing to contribute to the new employer. Don't put the spotlight on the reasons that you don't think that you are a good fit for the job but instead focus on your strengths not your weaknesses. Try and keep your personal life outside of the interview as bringing this up during an interview could make things uncomfortable during the interview.

Questions to Ask in an Interview.

It is a good idea to have a few questions for your interviewer even though you really just want to get out of the hot seat and end the interview as quickly as possible. Below are a couple of good questions to ask your interviewer during your job interview.

1) "How is success defined in this particular job?"

2) Ask a specific question about the organization to show that you did your homework on the company.

3) "Can I have a tour of the facilities?" This will show the interviewer that you are taking a vested interest in the company.

4) "What do you like the most about working here?" This will give you a chance to find out some of the perks to the job.

5) "Do you know of any reason why I might not get this job?" This will give you a chance to find out if the interviewer thinks you are a good candidate for the job. It can also give you a chance to straighten out and misconceptions they may have about you.

Chapter 7: How Important Is It To Look Good In An Interview?

Believe it or not, a job interview is considered one of the most stressful moments of your life. If you're a first timer and you need to engage in a one on one talk with an interviewer, the stress can be overwhelming. It's natural to feel uneasy or anxious each time you find yourself standing in front of a panel or a person who will try to throw you some questions that can make you feel uncomfortable. But that's how things go when you're trying to seek employment, you need to undergo some process which an employer has the right to put you in a hot seat.

A job interview is actually the best way to know if an applicant is suitable for the job. True enough, an employer will not invest time and money if they find the person applying for their job vacancy not qualified. That's why it's always been a standard office procedure or SOP among office establishment aside from a series of test to hold a personal interview with the applicant. Now, since you are applying for the job, you also need to do something to become worthy to your future employer. One particular area that you should look into is "how important to look good during the interview". If you think this is a simple subject that anyone can accomplish easily, well, it's not, but if you do it right, the result is very rewarding.

Why your personal representation is important when attending a job interview.

Here are three essential factors;

First impression – It's pretty obvious when it comes to engaging yourself to people, especially on a first time basis, first impression really lasts. This is very crucial when it comes to work interview. Employer needs a good reason to hire you. Therefore, if you come in late to your initial interview, even your interviewer would say it's fine, well the truth is, it's not. Why will the company hire someone who comes to work late? Next, if you don't look your best, like dressing up for the occasion. No employer will believe that you are somebody perfect for the job position if you don't look professional enough. Physical appearance adds up to your chance to get the job.

Persuasion — nothing beats a successful job interview for a person who owns a talent in persuasion. Remember, one of the best assets to nail a job interview is the power of persuasion. Even though you are confident to take the interview, but you are not persuasive enough to become suitable for the job, you can expect to read another job opening on the internet. Persuasion is the talent that anyone should have. A "Sweet tongue" can deliver powerful results to any conversation. It will help you build a good rapport towards your interviewer on the first 30 seconds that you're talking with your hiring manager. You know you are persuasive when you can make your audience agree with your opinion, even you know you're just making fun out of it.

Being presentable – You can dictate how people will treat you. This is a fact that you should really understand. Even if your qualifications are highly commendable for the job, but if you don't represent yourself well, the chances of landing the job is absolutely zero. There are times that an interviewer will not mind your presence because you don't look appealing. In fact, she/he will have the tendency to finish off the interview instantly and will tell the applicant these three famous lines "We'll call you".

Just keep this in mind. Job hunting is a serious matter. You're putting all your efforts to nail a job so try considering these 3 powerful bits of information.

Chapter 8: Presentation - Discovery

As we stated in chapter 3, the Discovery stage has the same ultimate purpose as the preparation stage, to uncover the felt need of the interviewers. In an ideal situation our efforts during the Discovery stage will confirm that one of the needs is in fact the felt need of our interviewer.

So we are looking to confirm our assumptions about their felt need through friendly conversation. But you must not be so focused on confirming your preparation that you overlook the possibility that their felt need is different than what you prepared for. If you miss the target and present yourself in a way that doesn't emotionally connect with your interviewers then your presentation will most likely fall flat and you will not get the job.

Here are some example Discovery Questions that are good for you to ask during the Discovery stage:

Tell me a bit about your vision for this department?

What motivates you to perform well?

What are some of your career goals?

How does this job I am applying for impact your goals?

In reality, just about any question which gets them talking about their fears and dreams for their career is a good question. If they balk a bit at you asking such questions just explain that you are looking to work for someone with a compelling or inspirational vision.

A challenge with the job interview that other sales meetings don't have is that the interviewers believe they are driving the meeting and in their minds it is not a sales meeting at all! Therefore, you will have to go through the discovery process in a give and take manner that allows you to ask thoughtful questions (so that you can confirm their felt need) while still answering the questions that they pose to you.

A simple outline of the Discovery stage is this:

Rapport building - Basic back and forth conversation about who you are and who they are to hopefully find common interests and passions.

Question & Answer -Interweave their questions about your resume and experience with your questions toward them designed to confirm or discover their felt need.

Identify the felt need, then seize the moment.

During rapport building you're trying to "hit it off" with the interviewers. Maybe you can make them laugh, maybe you have a common friend or acquaintance (who you both presumably like). Maybe you both like rock climbing. Maybe your kids are the same age. You're just hoping for some sort of connection with the human element. Time is limited in an interview setting. You might be their 9th interview of the day. They will likely want to move on quickly from this. Don't take it personally. Try your best. It's a great advantage if you find a connection, but it's not the end of the world if you don't.

During the Question & Answer portion of the meeting they will ask you all of the standard interview questions. Why do you want to work for us? How long did you work for such and such company? What were your responsibilities in your previous job? Why is there a two year gap in your resume? Tell us about a time you experienced workplace conflict.

You should have prepared answers for these questions that you are able to give easily and without sounding canned. But in between their questions try to ask the Discovery questions you prepared beforehand that seek to confirm their felt need. Rehearse your answers and your questions and try to make all of it seem as natural as possible.

You should come across as genuinely interested in them as people when asking questions. If you are not genuinely interested in them, you should become genuinely interested in them. You never know, they may become your greatest mentors or your biggest cheerleaders of your entire career.

Chapter 9: How To Fill Out Application Forms Correctly

Prior to interview, you'll be asked to fill out an application form. Although it seems trivial, the way you fill out the form will affect your overall test score. If you fill it out carelessly, you'll be considered a sloppy person.

Application forms provide background information needed by the company. Below is a list of common questions asked in the application form:

1) Name. Write down or insert your full name.

2) Address. Write down your full address including phone numbers.

3) ID/Driving License number. Write down your ID/Driving License number.

4) Position. Write down the position you are applying for.

5) Family. Write down the names of your family members, from father, mother, siblings, spouse (if any), and children (if any), including their age, educational level and addresses.

6) Education. Write down your educational history including college/school names, cities, graduation year or duration of studies, major/subject, and achievements.

7) Extracurricular activities. Write down the extracurricular activities you participated in at school or college.

8) Organizational activities. Write down the name, year and location of organizations you have been a member of.

9) Courses/seminars/workshops. Write down the names of courses/seminars/workshops you have attended, including the theme, organizer, location, and year.

10) Work experience. Write down your work experience, including company

names, position, year, salary, city, reason for moving.

11) Medical record. Write down your medical history. Whether you have undergone surgery, hospitalization, and so on.

12) Expected salary. Write down your expected salary. If you're a fresh graduate, it is recommended not to put a nominal value here. Just write that you expect your salary to be in line with the company's policy and commensurate with your skills and qualifications. This is to avoid asking for a salary that is too high or too low, which may put you at a disadvantage.

13) Readiness to work. If you're currently unemployed, write down as soon as possible or as needed by the company. If you're still employed, just write down I need to give 2-weeks' or 30-days' notice.

14) Are you willing to relocate? Answer "Yes" to this question. Even if you answered "Yes", it doesn't mean that you will be immediately assigned out of town.

This is only a test question to gauge your commitment and dedication, so fear not.

15) References. Write down the names of people who know you professionally. It would be better if they have a good reputation in a field that is relevant to the position you are applying for. They could be former or current coworkers or supervisors for experienced candidates or former lecturers or teachers for fresh graduates.

16) Are you willing to undergo a probationary period? Answer "Yes" to this question.

17) Why are you applying for this position? Give a positive answer to this question such as to advance your career, or because it is in line with your interests or educational background.

18) What are your hobbies? Write down your hobbies.

19) Are you willing to work out of town? Answer "Yes" to this question.

20) Are you willing to work overtime? Answer "Yes" to this question.

Application forms vary from company to company. Some companies may not ask all of these questions in the application form. Some may save them for the interview. But, one thing for sure is that you will be asked most of these questions at some point in the hiring process.

Make sure your writing is readable and neat. Read and answer each question carefully. Don't forget to write down your name and sign it.

Chapter 10: Pre-Interview Preparation: Details Of Your Story

Most questions you will be asked to answer during a typical job interview will be behavioral style questions (see Chapters 7 and 8 for more on interview questions), and the best way of preparing for these kinds of questions is to think of your previous professional (or educational) experience as an opportunity to put together a kind of story. The best interviews are ones that incorporate stories within a clear framework of what you have to offer to the position and to the company. As such, you should always be prepared when an interviewer asks you the simple (but potentially intimidating) question: what did you do when...? Or, how would you approach…? These open-ended questions practically beg you to tell a coherent story, rather than simply drop a set of vague characteristics that you might possess or amorphous hypotheticals that don't reveal anything specific about yourself or your abilities. These open-ended questions will inevitably crop up and being prepared for them requires you to think in advance about how you might present yourself in the story: preparing an outline and underscoring characteristics that reveal your value as an employee is a powerful way to impress an interviewer both with your skills and with your poise—as well as to reveal a cohesive narrative about who you are as a valuable employee.

As stated above, these kinds of questions are called behavioral interview questions ("Tell me about a time when you made a mistake"); they are designed to allow you to reveal behavioral characteristics that show strengths and abilities that can be applied to workplace scenarios. (For more on types of interview questions, see Chapters 7 and 8, or for an in-depth exploration of these themes, see my book **Interview Q&A**.) The best way to handle these kinds of questions is to be prepared in advance with at least a couple of stories that you have spent some time outlining. The interviewer wants a specific answer, not a meandering and vague recitation of how your leadership skills helped you out. Additionally, the interviewer is interested in your response to a situation—your behavior, your **actions**—rather than a passive recitation of generalized qualities.

Your first response should be concise and direct: "One of the most memorable professional mistakes I made was when XXX happened." Thus, you clearly indicate to the interviewer that you understand the question and give them a basis for following your story. Then, fill in the context: briefly indicate the background surrounding the event, what the consequences were, and then give details as to how you specifically handled it—and, ideally, what you learned from it, as well.

Always be certain to explain your role in the process honestly and thoroughly; there is no need to assign or deflect blame. The interviewer is trying to determine how you might respond to a difficult situation, not to assess your perfection or lack thereof. The more honest and genuine you are, the more you reveal the strength of character and a willingness to learn.

In addition, be certain that you provide some specific details: what exact steps did you take to remedy the situation, and what particular qualities in you did those actions reveal? The more detailed (though not long-winded) you are about your role, the more you address the specifics of your overall character and qualification for the position. In fact, specificity is truly one of the keys to conducting a successful job interview—or job hunt overall—and landing your ideal job. This applies to your resume and cover letter, as well; the more specific each component of your job search is, the more successful your candidacy. This means tailoring each component of your interview (and resume and cover letter) to each specific job applied for; this shows an enthusiasm that cannot be expressed simply via experience.

Elaborate on the end results of your story and, particularly, be sure to point out what you learned from the particular event. Especially if you are asked to recount a negative event from your professional history, like a mistake, you want to assure the interviewer that, rather than seeing it as a failure, you viewed it as a learning opportunity, one that allowed you to develop certain skills more fully. The importance of stories in any setting is that they reveal common ground among people and allow for emotional connection: the more familiar you are with the hero of your story (that would be you) and the motivations for your actions, the more genuine and emotionally personable you come across. For that reason, good storytelling requires some advance preparation and practice.

Before you begin to prepare your story, remember that the most effective stories in an interview setting will have the following qualities: the story should be simple and straightforward; it should be unique to you with an unexpected detail or two; it should be clear and concrete in its details; it should seem credible and genuine (this is **not** the time for fiction!); and it should create some sort of emotional connection.

Even if you feel skilled at answering questions "off the cuff," as it were, it will benefit you to spend some time with your story before an interview. Create an outline that would serve you for any number of stories:

Give your story a name, which serves as an anchor of the overarching topic.

Identify the problem or opportunity the story presents.

Identify the players within the story. You should be the main character, of course, but clearly note who else was involved and how.

Relay the central action of the story: what happened and why.

Convey the results of the action: what followed from the central action and what was its impact.

Identify what competencies this story reveals about its hero (you).

Identify what characteristics this story reveals about its hero (you).

Determine what about the story is unexpected.

Competencies are skills that you possess that are valuable to the interviewer and employer. The most common competencies identified by prospective employers are that of leadership, problem-solving, teamwork, management or organization, communication, and customer-focused. Highlight one or more of these skills within the context of your story.

Characteristics are traits that you possess that are valuable to the interviewer and employer. The most common character traits identified by employers are honesty, passion, confidence, motivation, reliability, and efficiency. Highlight one or more of these skills within the context of your story.

The unexpected may be one of the hardest things to discover within your story, but it important to create some interest in the listener, especially considering that he or she has likely listened to more than one interview during the course of a day or a week; you want to stand out somehow. You can find unexpectedness in several places: the action itself could arise from something that is unusual or unanticipated; the characters involved could be unusual (an outsider is somehow involved, or a quirky colleague); the response to the action could be risky or innovative; the result was surprisingly efficient or positive; or, the original approach was scrapped in favor of something new and daring. Finding the unexpected creates greater interest in your story—a hook, as it were. Consider using STAR guidelines to help you outline your story: Situation, Task, Action, and Result (see Chapters 9 and 10 for a more in-depth discussion of answering interview questions, including the STAR technique). This will keep you on track and focused on the importance of the story as a whole.

Even with all this preparation, you don't want to sound too rehearsed. First, you cannot anticipate the specific question that an interviewer might ask that would prompt a story, and if you answer with a canned response that doesn't quite fit the question, this is awkward and can seem disingenuous. This is why having two or three various stories that could be used to answer a variety of behavioral questions is most effective. Make sure you know the details and keep your story focused: practice so much that, instead of sounding rote, it rolls off the tongue like a spur-of-the-moment response. Don't write the story itself out and memorize a script;

instead, memorize the outline and follow it to tell a naturally evolving story.

As with many aspects of your job search, certain components are somewhat consistent, such as the kinds of questions or prompts that frequently come up in interview situations. Again, this will be covered in more detail later in this guide, but here are some that are particularly well suited to putting together a cohesive story. Some particular kinds of stories that are always good to have ready to relay are as follows:

Be prepared to "tell a little about yourself." Most people don't bother with spending any time with that, but it often leads to rambling and incoherent responses. Instead, use some of the ideas above to reveal something relevant about yourself in light of this position: the best idea is to keep it a short one-minute synopsis of what makes you the ideal candidate for the job.

As in the example above, being asked to tell about the time you made a mistake is a classic interview question and can reveal a lot about you as a candidate. Even a disastrous story wherein you learned a valuable lesson could showcase your tenacity, determination, and flexibility—as well as creative thinking and problem-solving.

Prepare a story about teamwork: showcasing your ability to work with others in positive and productive ways is key in many, if not most, work situations. Support and teamwork are just as important, if not more so than leadership and individual initiative.

Talk about a particular challenge you have faced in your professional life (or personal, if it can be made relevant) and how you confronted it and dealt with it. Overcoming obstacles is one of the core actions that reveal our deepest personality characteristics; additionally, these stories also offer a chance to make a lasting emotional connection with the listener.

You might also relate a story about a time that you showed impressive leadership skills. Even if you are just now embarking on your career, you should be able to come up with a story wherein you took the lead in creating something meaningful or fixing a problem.

Problem-solving also gives you an opportunity to reveal your professional and personal qualities. Tell a story about a time you resolved a complex problem and what skills you used in order to do so.

There is also room in storytelling to reveal something more personal about yourself, especially in today's marketplace and within certain industries. "Tell me what you are passionate about" is a more common prompt than not in interview settings today. Find a way to tell a story about your passions and dearest interests that apply to the position for which you are interviewing.

Finally, there are occasionally appropriate moments during which you can tell a story about what you do for fun, or for a hobby—things that are important to you personally. The purpose of telling such stories—and of the interviewer asking more personal questions—is to reveal particular traits that highlight who you are. For example, if you enjoy gardening, you could tell a story about the challenges and joys of overcoming weather and pests to harvest some homegrown food for your family. This kind of story says a lot about perseverance.

Telling stories about our experiences and ourselves is a way to humanize a sometimes sterile interview setting. Storytelling creates emotional connections and reveals more about you than the bullet points on your resume. Make these stories count by thinking them through and organizing them prior to your interview. If they are genuine, unexpected, and thoughtful, they will invariably become some of the most memorable things about you. Don't be afraid to be your genuine self, though always with a professional and practiced poise.

Chapter 11: The Perfect Attire

What you wear is, of course, a huge part of your first impression. They say you should dress for the job you want, not the job you have. This is absolutely true when you go to an interview.

Many people think that they must wear a suit to any interview they go to. While a suit does show that you are serious about the job, it is sometimes unnecessary. This is where researching the company and position can come in handy.

You never want to be dressed more professionally than your interviewer, if at all possible. If you are interviewing for a position in a very casual office, you want to be dressed business-casual. For men this means slacks, a nice button up shirt, and perhaps a tie. No suit coat needed. For women this means a simple skirt and professional blouse or sweater. You could also wear a simple pair of slacks.

If you are going to be working somewhere where jeans are the norm, there is nothing wrong with wearing jeans to the interview. However, be absolutely certain that this is the case. You should not wear jeans unless you are positive that the interviewer will also be wearing jeans.

If you are interviewing for a more professional position you should wear a suit. Women can wear a dress suit, a professionally cut dress, or a professional skirt and blouse. Men should wear slacks, shirt, tie and jacket. In a slightly less formal setting you can dismiss the tie.

You should never wear tennis shoes to an interview. Men should wear loafers or dress shoes. Women can wear a nice pair of sandals in the summer, or they can wear dress shoes. It is important not to wear shoes that are uncomfortable or painful to wear. Women may want to avoid high heels. You want to be as comfortable as possible to avoid fidgeting during the interview. Never wear flashy shoes such as you would wear to a club.

It is helpful to do some research into the culture of the company before your interview to know how to dress for it. If you know someone who works there ask them about the average daily attire. If you live nearby and can do so easily you might visit the office anonymously so you can see for yourself how people are dressed. If this is not possible, try visiting their website. If they have pictures of their office you can get an idea of how people dress based on the pictures.

When in doubt, go with business casual, unless you are interviewing for an obviously professional position. If you are interviewing for a management position, or a position such as a lawyer's assistant, you should dress the part in a more formal attire. Business casual tends to be the norm in today's office culture. It is very rare for an office to require formal attire of its employees, and therefore business casual is perfect for an interview for these positions.

Etiquettes and Body Language Required in an Interview

You should use proper etiquette in an interview. Always use basic manners, such as please and thank you. You should appear as professional as possible at all times.

Always start the interview by thanking the interviewer for their time, and let them know how happy you are to be there. You should then show excellent listening skills to all questions by showing that you are paying attention. Tilt your head a bit to show interest, and maintain eye contact.

Answer all questions truthfully and in an easy manner. This is where your practice of interview questions comes in handy. You should be able to have an easy conversation with your interviewer. This is not just a time for them to ask you questions that they ask everyone. It is a time for them to get to know you. You do not want to have them get one impression of you, then discover you are entirely different upon hire. That could lose you the job quickly and waste everyone's time. While you should be professional, it is also important to be yourself.

Body language can sometimes say more about you than the words you speak. You should not fidget at all during an interview. Do not play with your jewelry, ring your hands, tap your foot, mess with your hair, or constantly straighten your clothing. Fidgeting in this way takes the attention of the interviewer away from what you are saying. It also shows that you are nervous and unprepared for the interview.

It is very tempting for some people to talk with their hands. People most often do this when they are excited about something, or very passionate about what they are saying. While this attitude is something that interviewers look for, talking with your hands in constant motion is also distracting for the interviewer. Try to keep this motion at a minimum.

How you sit is also important. You should sit with good posture, with your back straight and your feet planted on the floor. You may want to sit cross legged, with one leg over the other. For women this is typically acceptable when you are wearing a skirt, and is considered lady like. For men it is a much more casual posture that is not typically suitable for an interview or the work place, and should be avoided.

You should have good posture, but at the same time give the impression that you are an open book and comfortable in the conversation. Often when people are nervous they hunch their shoulders, tie their hands in their lap, and appear to be trying to escape into themselves. This is a horrible impression to make.

Instead, try sitting with your arms on the arms of the chair. If the chair does not have arms, place your hands loosely in your lap. Do not grip the arms of the chair, and do not let your arms dangle lifelessly. A comfortable, casual posture is important. Not only will this make you more comfortable with the interview and better able to remember all of your preparation, it will also make you appear confident and open to any question that the interviewer might answer.

An open posture also gives the interviewer the impression that you are completely open and honest about all of your answers. It shows that you have nothing to hide, and that you are willing to answer anything they have to throw at you. People with open postures tend to be more trustworthy.

At the beginning of the interview you should introduce yourself and shake the interviewer's hand. At the end of the interview you should shake their hand again and thank them for their time, telling them that it was a pleasure to meet them. A good hand shake is important.

You do not want someone to feel like you are trying to break their hand when you shake it. A firm handshake is important, but too firm is a bad thing. Before shaking someone's hand try to size them up. Women are going to have a lighter touch and grip, and you should not shake their hand with a very firm grip. Men will have a firmer grip and you can respond with the same. Your grip should be firm but pliant. This shows that you are both confident and comfortable with the meeting.

While in an interview you should have your phone turned off completely. Most phones vibrate loudly and can still be a distraction. Turn off the sound all the way, or turn the phone off. This way your interview will not be interrupted. Having your phone on, and especially answering your phone, during an interview is considered very rude and will definitely lose the job for you. If you are concerned about your ability to leave your phone alone do not take it in with you at all.

What to Carry in an Interview

You should carry as little as possible into an interview. Your hands should be free to shake the hand of your interviewer. You should also avoid having anything in your hands to play with that will distract you or make you fidget during the interview.

You should definitely carry in a clean, unfolded copy of your resume. While you likely provided your resume during the application process, you should assume that the interviewer may want a clean copy for their review. In addition if there is more than one interviewer in the room, each may want their own copy of your resume. Even if it is not used by the interviewer, it is best to be prepared in the case that they want it to review. If they do not use it, you can refer to it yourself to help you answer questions.

If you are interviewing for a professional position you may also want to take in a portfolio of your educational credentials, professional licenses, and awards you may have earned. You can also include examples of your work if you are interviewing for a position as a marketer or other job where you can easily show paper examples of what you can do for the company.

Any portfolio you carry in with you should be professional in appearance. Do not carry in a simple manila folder, a colored folder, or loose papers. A leather folder or binder is best. You can also get basic brown cardboard portfolios. A nice report portfolio is also acceptable. Alternatively you can use a clean, plain white or black binder with your credentials and licenses included within in clean and clear sheet protectors.

If you drove your car you will likely be carrying keys into the building. Put your keys in your pocket or purse so that they are out of sight and out of your hands. If you are not carrying a purse and have no pockets, lay the keys down on the table or desk in front of you.

Women may or may not want to carry a purse into an interview. You might want to carry your purse to keep from leaving it exposed in the car. If you used public transportation you will have to have your purse on you by necessity. If you have loose keys and no where to put them you may also want to carry a purse. However, if you can avoid it, it is good to leave your purse behind. It is simply one more thing there that could distract you, and one more thing you have to remember to grab when you leave.

You should not take your phone into your interview if you can help it. If you can leave it in the car, do so. If this is not possible or you used public transportation, make sure your phone is turned off and put away in a pocket or in your purse.

If you need a place to keep your phone and keys and also have a portfolio to share, a small briefcase or professional tote might be in order. This way you can carry all of the things you need in one hand, and it will appear professional rather than unnecessary bulk.

How to Create a Resume

You will need to create a resume before applying for jobs. However, you will also need to carry this resume with you into an interview. Be prepared to use your resume for any purpose by having a well-organized, formatted copy of your resume at hand at all times.

Creating a resume is fairly simple. You can find resume creators and templates all over the internet. Most word processing software comes with built in resume templates. If you are not great with formatting, these templates are often your best bet.

However, there is much more to creating a resume than format. You will need to know what to include in your resume to help you get noticed and hired. This is sometimes the most difficult part of creating a resume.

It is helpful to create a general resume that can be used for all positions that you apply for. This gives you a starting point, and a document that can be easily accessed and forwarded to potential employers. However, it can also be helpful to be able to change this document as needed to tailor it to a specific position or company.

Types of Resumes

There are two types of resumes. You can organize your resume chronologically, which is the most common way that people tend to automatically format their resume. Your other option is to create a functional resume.

A chronological resume may have a section that lists your education, a section that lists your skills, and a section that lists your work experience. The bulk of the resume is your work experience, listed in chronological order starting with your current or most recent position. You can include a brief description of your position for each entry in the work experience section.

A functional resume focuses more on your abilities than your experience. A functional resume is preferred if you are a recent college graduate just entering the work force in your chosen career field. The functional resume focuses more on your education, skills and accomplishments. In a functional resume you may create more of a description of the skills and talents you obtained through your educational experiences. You may also have a section listing specific career related accomplishments, and a section for skills and talents. You will still need to include your brief work history, but this is done at the end of the resume with only a listing of position, company and dates of employment. The work history portion of the functional resume is almost an afterthought.

Chapter 12: Give Your Interview The Right Closing

Most people introduce themselves perfectly and are impeccably prepared for their interviews. However, they do not realize that the decision on their hiring is made right after they leave. This makes a good closing a crucial part of the interview process. You can wipe of all your efforts by simply making a bad closing to the interview. Here are a few tips on what you can do:

Ask questions.

Leave the interviewer(s) with three things that you would like them to recollect about you.

Prepare addresses early to help you choose if the position is suitable for you.

Remain eager and gracious.

This is likewise a chance to give extra data about your experience that you think is vital to the position and that was not secured in the meeting. You must also ask relevant questions at the end to show your eagerness and interest in the job. Some questions that you can consider include:

Are there are any critical aptitudes required for the employment that have not been secured in the meeting?

What do you need the individual in this position to fulfill inside the initial three months?

What is the time allotment for settling on the procuring choice?

On the contrary, there are some questions that you must keep away from asking. These are:

What are the organization profits, excursion arrangements or different advantages of the occupation?

What is the pay at the beginning?

These subjects can be tricky, and you must wait for the questioner to present these subjects. The best time to discuss compensation is after you have been offered the occupation. You are then in a greatly improved position to arrange.

Ideally, an interview ends when one or more interviewers stand up. You must not consider an interview as ended until this time, or unless you are advised on this by one of the interviewers. You must conclude the interview with:

During the meeting or not long after, record the name(s) of the interviewer(s) so you won't overlook.

Shake hands and thank him/her for thinking of you as a prospective employee.

Chapter 13: Getting Into Interview State

The very prospect of an imminent job interview is enough to give many people sleepless nights and cold sweats. Nobody likes to be on the receiving end of what seems like a firing squad. Chances are, if you are unable to overcome your nerves on the interview day, the hiring manager will be able to smell it and judge you based on that.

Truthfully, most hiring managers are not out there to make people like you miserable during the interview. They do their part in assessing the person by asking certain kinds of question. What you simply have to do is to provide them with the answers they are looking for. To do this, you will first need to change your mindset.

Do not think of the interview as an intense period of questioning and interrogation. While it is partially true to some extent, interviews are also a chance for you to make judgments about the companies as well. It is your only chance to find out if the company is a right fit for you and you have to adopt this mindset. Once you can achieve this, you will regain the sense of control, which is often lost as soon as people enter the interview room. Interview is a two-way communication between yourself and the company.

You also want to be prepared for the interview as discussed in the previous chapter. Being prepared not only serve to empower you with the knowledge to sail through the interview smoothly, it also helps to calm your nerves. Simply knowing the fact that you are prepared for the interview alone is good enough to reduce your anxiety. To achieve this, you will not only want to research about the company, but also prepare confident answers to obvious questions as well as a set of great questions to ask the interviewer in return. All of these will be discussed about in later chapters.

You also want to be prepared for your schedule on the day of the interview. Plan out your route to the location of your interview a few days before and always reach your interview location 15-30 minutes before the interview starts. Punctuality speaks volume on your habits and personality and you do not want the possibility of reaching late to wreck your nerves just before the interview. Having to hurry will only leave you feeling flustered and anxious. Decide what to wear the night before and then get an early night! It may be a good idea to take a sleeping remedy to ensure you get a full night's sleep.

At the end of the interview, exit as if this is a personal success: show a confident and assured smile and give a firm handshake. Some of this confidence is bound to transfer across to the interviewer and this will help you leave a positive last impression of yourself. Regardless of the success of the interview, you want to put it away to the back of your mind the moment you leave the interview location. Your joy or worries will have no effect on the next interviews you might be attending. Dwelling too much on your past performance can negatively impact your next interviews if you have any. They are a source of distraction. What you need to do is to draw experience from what you have learned coming out of that interview and lay it as a good foundation to build your next interview preparation upon. Even if you have failed this time, it has still provided excellent practice.

Chapter 14: Top Job Interview Questions

Are you too qualified for this job?

If you encounter this question during your job interview, you may find yourself feeling immediately frustrated. This can happen especially for older workers because you may feel that they think you're too old for this job. However, this question comes up because companies don't want to make a mistake in hiring. They don't want to hire someone that will move on to a higher paying job as soon as it is available. They understand that you will take the opportunity to have a higher paying better position.

When someone asks you if you're overqualified, you need to look beyond the question to something more. They're asking if you're going to be bored, if this is the right position for you, and if you're going to be satisfied here.

All of this boils down to the overarching question of, "Are you a good fit for this job?" This is the question that you should be answering. They'll want to know that they're making a good decision by picking you for this job. If you make them feel better about picking you, then you'll definitely have caught their attention.

If you get asked this question, then here are a couple of ways to answer.

"I might be too qualified, but wouldn't that be wonderful? You would have someone in the position that's done this before. You would have someone that already understands what it takes to be successful." This calls back to the four questions that you need to be answering with every answer you give: Do you understand the job? Are you able to do this job? Will you do this job? Are you going to be a threat to their continued employment?

Another answer could be, "I am overqualified for this position; however, this position looks wonderful to me because of A, B, and C." These three reasons are going to be the personal reasons why this job fits you. These reasons should go beyond money, responsibilities, or advancement possibilities. These reasons could be literally anything that matters to you. It could even be as simple as a shorter commute. I met a man once that had such a reason. He told them his reasons up front. He had a paid off home, he didn't need tons of extra money, and he liked where he lived. After getting across the point that he had, the company was excited about hiring him.

The key is explaining why the company and the job is perfect for you. Those that are doing the hiring might not understand exactly what you see on their own. They'll make assumptions, which isn't good news for you. Instead of letting them make those assumptions, you should be attempting to help them out by explaining your reasoning up front.

Will you relocate for this position?

This can be very a common question when you're interviewing. There are times where this can break deals, but there are times when it won't. Even if it isn't necessary for you to move, the flexibility can be important for long-term growth. Most people feel the need to immediately answer with something along the lines of, "I would consider moving for the right job."

This isn't the answer that you want to give, even if it's true. You will want to avoid this answer because it will make it look like you are ready to move for the right amount of money. This will make the interview see you as someone that's more interested in the money. This is a small thing, but it can really affect how you are viewed.

You will need to have a couple ways to deal with the situation, regardless of what kind of answer you want to give. So we'll be going over how you should answer depending on what your overall thoughts are.

If you are unwilling to relocate, you need to say that. However, remember that life changes unexpectedly. You might be unwilling to move right now, but something could change tomorrow that would make you much more willing to relocate. Life can change rather quickly.

A good answer for being unwilling to relocate might something along the lines of, "I would rather not move at the moment, but life can change quickly. And I'm really interested in both the position and this company."

If you're on the fence about moving, you might not be willing to commit to packing up your life, even if this job is a great opportunity. To be perfectly honest, many people don't want to move. Your family situation, your friends, and a number of other things are in this place. However, you'd be willing to consider relocating for the right offer.

We've already gone over the fact that you can't answer them like that. Instead, you should say something like, "I'm very interested in working on growing my career. If relocating is necessary for that growth, then, of course, I would consider it." This means that you won't be committed to moving, but you think that the job and your career are important.

You could also say something along the lines of, "Where I live isn't the most important issue for me. Being able to use my skills, develop new skills, and advancing my career are what really interest me. I'm convinced that this company, as well as this job, is a great fit because of the skills I possess, like X, Y, and Z. Wouldn't you agree?" This kind of response is on track, pushes that you are the right person for the job, and redirects the conversation elsewhere.

You can always fall back on an answer like, "I would consider relocating." But you need to make sure that you have at least one answer that will be honest, tactful, and more reasonable than saying you would consider the move for the 'right opportunity.' You would keep the conversation moving in a positive direction.

Describe how your work was once criticized and how you handled the critique.

This question might make you feel terrified. It's not easy. However, this question can tell an interviewer a lot about you. From what situation you describe to the outcome, there is a lot of information that they can see through what you say. This question, in particular, can tell them a lot about how it would be to work with you. This is information that you can see through lists of qualifications and skills.

This is a question that you should always be prepared for. There have to be several situations that you can immediately think of when this kind of question is said. In order to be a good employee, you have to be open to critiques. This is important to situations outside of work as well. If you're not open to criticism, then you're going to be hard to coach.

Coachability is incredibly important, as is taking criticism. Both of these can show great things about you as an employee. If you can't take criticism, then you will be defensive and won't suck up any of the information that you are being offered. By not wanting to take more information in, you will be offered less information. You will also have fewer opportunities to improve your work. Eventually, you might find yourself fired.

This may sound extreme, however, if your boss can't correct you, then you're not going to do well. No one is perfect. Everyone needs some corrections to their work from time to time. This teaching can help make sure that you are improved.

That is coachability. So when you get this question, you will want to tell them about a time when someone tried to tell you how to do something a little different or a little better. You'll want to talk about how you responded to the advice, and what ended up happening. This is similar to the STAR system. Situation or Task, Action, and Result is what STAR stands for. Follow this structure and it will work well for this question.

When your workload has been heavy, what happened and how did you handle it?

Getting you to talk about a difficult situation is a common and favorite tactic that interviewers will use. This is another incidence of behavioral interviewing. These questions will dig deeper into what you are capable of. The way that you have acted in the past can help predict how you will react to future situations.

The interviewer wants you to know if you are the kind of person that blows up when things get bad. Everyone will eventually have a hard time. Different industries have different crunch times. Accountants to have the heaviest loads in March. Retailers suffer the most around Christmas. Even industries and companies that don't have seasonal crunch times can see crunch times throughout their time.

The answer to this question will help the interviewer see how you approach day-to-day problems. They want to know that you can handle it when your workload changes. If you are capable of adapting, then the answer to this question should show them that. You'll walk them through the situation and what you used to deal with it.

An example of an answer might sound like, "Everyone has times when their workloads are heavier. When I'm in that kind of situation, I have found that the best thing that I can do is prioritize tasks that I have to do. Typically there are tasks that aren't immediate concerns. Prioritize the tasks and then tackle what you have to do first."

Following this statement, you should tell the story of you dealt with the situation.

You should probably follow the STAR method when describing the situation.

You can also say something along the lines of, "In these high-stress situations, I look at the workload, prioritize critical tasks, then go to my supervisor and see if there are additional prioritization that I should be looking at. This allows me to feel more in control."

This kind of statement should be followed by a story of helping a boss. This will show that you are capable of working with someone to get through the situation.

You will want to avoid saying something along the lines of, "I stuck around until the work was done." This answer focuses just on the long hours that you worked in order to finish the crunch period successfully. Focusing on working with your employer and prioritizing their needs can make it apparent that you work hard and smart.

Don't avoid talking about the fact that you worked hard, but follow it up with more about yourself. Show the thought process that you went through. This can often show people how you will act in that particular job. It will also help you stand out from others since you will be focusing on how your decisions benefit the company.

How do you handle a situation where you are required to finish many tasks before the end of the day, but there is no way to finish every single task?

Job interviews have to be a little bit like speed dating. Instead of just focusing on your resume, a company will want to talk about real life situations that you have dealt with over the years. This will give them an idea of your skills beyond what you have written down. This is why they rely heavily on behavioral interviewing. You'll want to be prepared for these questions before you even walk into the room.

This particular question is a very common question that people use for behavioral interviewing. It is an extremely common situation. This means that you don't have to get into specific situations when it comes to your answer. You'll need to go through your thought process because that's what they really want to get at.

Touch on how you approach problems, what tools you use to solve these problems, and how you prioritize. They'll want someone to not collapse under the pressure or explode in anger. Through your answer, you'll be able to show exactly how you look when you're under pressure.

There are some answers that you don't want to give like, "I expect that my boss will give me a reasonable workload. I also expect that they'll recognize that not everything will get done." Another bad example would be, "I would keep working until I finished everything, even if it meant staying really late."

The second answer might sound good, but it shows a lack of your ability to really think on your feet. You're not analyzing the situation and using a more reasonable solution.

Instead, focus on the prioritization process that you go through. What absolutely has to be done? In most situations, you have probably found that even if there are 20 tasks that need to be done, some of them can't be used right away. Over the next couple of days, they might only be able to get through 5 to 10 of them. So instead of getting buried under the sheer amount of work, you'll be able to focus on those first 5 to 10 that they need.

Show them that you are capable of strategizing the tasks and that will make you one of the more impressive interview candidates.

Describe how you work.

You might have heard something about work style. This is a really common kind of question, but there are many people that just don't know how to answer effectively. When it comes to this question, you'll want to avoid talking about your personality in this question. They just want to know how you get through the day.

You might feel tempted to say that you're laid back when it comes to work, but this answer will really just work against you. Being laid back is really a personality trait, and it's not a necessarily desirable trait when it comes to work. No one wants an employee that just kind of meanders around at work. They want to make sure that you're going to give them the most for their money.

You'll also want to avoid saying that you're not a fan of conflict. This doesn't really have a lot to do with your work style. This answer doesn't really tell the interviewer anything about your work style.

For a good answer, there are a couple things you will want to do. You will want the answer that you give to mesh with the job that you're applying for. If you've got a very straight forward, data-driven position, then you won't want to spend time talking about the creative solutions that you're able to come up with. It isn't a necessary trait for your job.

You'll want to address whether you like to work in groups or by yourself. You might have an actual preference, but you'll also want to address what this particular job requires of you. Being able to work both alone and with someone else can be a great bonus for most companies. Talk about how comfortable with both.

You'll also want to tell them about how much instruction you need on jobs. This is something that you should be upfront with, especially if you tend to only function well with a lot of instruction or very little instruction. This can help see if this job will be a good fit for you. The boss might be on the other side of the spectrum from you. Without being upfront, you could be stuck in a job where you aren't able to function at your most effective.

With this kind of question, you'll want to touch on the strengths you have that fit well with this job. You might talk about organization, planning, performance, and more. These are just ideas to get you thinking. Regardless of the exact answer, you will want to approach these questions with a prepared, strategic answer that will not only address the question, but that will touch on other parts of your personality and work style that make you a good fit for the job.

Chapter 15: Steps To Take After Your Interview

☐If you don't hear from the company, you interviewed with after a set amount of time, call them or send an email. Find out if the process is complete. Are they still reviewing applicants? This let's let them know you are still available and interested.

☐If your rejected, don't be disappointed or discouraged. Think of it as practice for the next interview. Think back and try to figure out where you feel like you lost them. It may not even be anything you did wrong. It may simply be that another candidate had more experience. It may even be, dare I say this? They already had a candidate in mind and due to the laws of non-discrimination had to go through the motions of interviewing applicants. So, for those reasons don't give up on your job search just let it be a confidence building practice exercise.

☐ If you got the job. Awesome, congrats! Finalize any questions or information you wish you had asked about during the interview.

☐ Make sure you are clear on where you go for the first day, who you are meeting up with.

☐ Send a thank you note for the interview or the job offer when it happens. Not a text, a typed letter mailed the old fashion way will stand out. However, if that is not an option at least a thank you email. It doesn't have to be several pages long. Keep it simple.

☐ One other little piece of advice. Don't join in the office or break room gossip. Especially the first week. Take time to learn who is trustworthy and who is not. Remember those gossiping about others are also sharing any personal information they learn about you with everyone else. You never know if that person also applied for the position and is disappointed you are working in that spot rather than them.

So make acquaintances but keep sharp until you learn who is who and what is what for yourself.

☐I am giving you an example of a sample letter to use as a guide. Feel free to tweak and change it to better fit the company or business you are going to work with.

Chapter 16: Prepare For The Interview

Preparing for the interview is as important and equally significant as the actual interview process itself. You need to take in consideration all possible parameters and be prepared as much as possible prior to the interview. Having the answers and solutions for anything that will be needed prior to the interview will eliminate all the feelings of uncertainty and insecurity.

Now let's take all options one by one in order to be 100% confident that you are ready for your interview.

1.Prepare for your travel.

•Are you familiar with the location of the company's building?

•Are there any major construction work taking place or happening near the company's building or to the routes leading there?

- The route which you have in mind using does it tend to have a lot of traffic on the hours or near the hours of your scheduled appointment?

- How long it will take you to drive there? If you are using other means of transportation like Taxi, bus or train how long it will take you to get there by using them?

- Does the area offer or the company provide any side parking or you will have to find one?

2.Prepare print copies of:

- Your resume

- Your professional references

3.Check the weather forecast for any weather conditions that may affect or delay your travel to destination.

4.Practice general answers to likely questions (In Section 4 will provide and go over the most common interview questions along with answers). Tailor these answers so that they reflect upon the needs of the company and job position you are applying for. You can even practice with a friend or a family member. If you are scheduled for a web interview you can practice in front of a camera.

5.Prepare success stories from your past to present and share in case being asked, such as an occasion from your previous company which your team was very close missing an important deadline and you have stepped in providing an alternative solution and help out both the team and the company to achieve the goal.

6.Stay and look healthy. People who look healthier inspire more confidence than those who seem to be poor in health. You can accomplish this by following the below pointers:

•Get plenty of sleep!!! Clear eyes demonstrate alertness and focus while on the other hand bloodshot eyes and dark circles under the eyes send a bad and negative message.

•Drink plenty of water and eat a good diet. This will make your body to feel better and produce healthy image. Water makes our body look clear and sharp.

•Avoid consumption of alcohol. If for any reason you get nervous and sweaty during the interview process then your body will first reject the alcohol and people around you could get the alcohol smell.

•Get a bit of physical exercise before the interview even if that is a 10 minute walk by your neighborhood or a few pushups or a swim by the pool. Taking few minutes to exercise will make your body project a sense and feeling of healthiness making you show healthier, energetic and confident.

Chapter 17: Salary Negotiation

Salary is the compensation for the services rendered. In the earlier pages we discussed about the components of pay, bifurcation and how it is fixed. Any employer is deemed to contribute basic benefits of employment. The sum up of compensation and benefits is figured in the total package. This is the total annual 'Cost-to-company' or CTC incurred by the employer towards that employee.

The percentage of fixed and variable pay will vary among companies. It is not always mandatory to have a variable pay. It depends upon the nature of business and the job position. Normally you enter the final round of salary negotiation to close the deal only after you get selected. Inspite of a fat annual package, if net pay per month is very low, candidates summarily reject it or never turn up to take offer. (Fixed and variable percentages as 70-30, 60-40 are failure models that have to be avoided for retention sake.)

Now, with fear of losing a good candidate, the HR department takes to the role of customer follow up only to be turned down by the candidate mercilessly. Many successful candidates who cleared the interview rounds either get rejected or pulled down in negotiation. It is up to organisation to restructure the percentage factor to attract candidates. Prepare in advance to show you are a good negotiator.

Asking for anything beyond the prevailing level is greedy. When they get trapped they least know that it is quick sand. Beyond a limit of satisfaction when negotiation fails, candidate is rejected as 'costly'.

Having worked hard to crack the interview, why should you slip down at negotiation stage? This does not happen only at the time of interview but also during appraisal interviews as well. Appraisal hike will not effect in all quarters of the year. It is based on Q1/2/3/4 finance report. Job hunters should get the following points clarified.

Is salary negotiable?

It is true that salary breakup percentage of components is not the same. Some allowances vary with the position level /grade. When annual CTC is spelled, it would appear to be big but blindly never divide upon 12 to arrive at monthly gross salary.

[If the range quoted is too high, then there is a possibility of negotiating on the lowest figure in range. So guess their mind and demand. It has become universal to fix CTC on fixed and variable components. If pay fixed is 60k, it could be as 48k fixed and 12k as variable. Will annual pay be realised at year end? After statutory deduction, take home pay comes to 45k or so. If the employee does not stay till year end, the chance of getting full variable pay is less. With random rating, negotiated CTC diminishes. It is mandatory to mark * as conditions apply.

If productivity is 100% then gross could appreciably go up. This practice is widely followed across industries. So fluctuation in salary is often observed. [A fresher has to accept whatever is offered as per the Minimum wages Act.] For example, let's see this CTC breakup. (This model is a rough working taken for clarity and discussion.) Gross minus Statutory deduction is **Net pay**. Net pay minus loan, fine, and liabilities is **Take home** pay.

Compensation Structure

Compensation head	INR Monthly	INR Annual
Fixed	40000	480000

Variable	20000	240000
CTC (cost to company)	60000	720000

Breakup of **Fixed pay**	Monthly
Basic	20000
HRA	8000
Conveyance	1600
Medical	2000
Phone	1000
Others	7400
Gross Salary	40000

Rating	Variable Pay
	140

			%
		5	100%
Breakup of **Variable pay**	INR Monthly	4	85%
Performance linked incentive (Rating based)	20000 ?	3	65%
		2	45%
Benefits (Employer contribution)		1	25%

EPF/ESIC/Bonus/ Over Time/ Gratuity/ Leave encashment/ Interest free loan /Wedding gift /Maternity pay/ ESOP/ Sponsored Training course / Group Insurance etc.

Deduction (Employee contribution)

EPF/ESIC/P-tax/TDS/LWF etc.

* Percentage breakup of fixed pay components varies with grade and title.

If an employee whose CTC is less and do not fall in tax range then HR can restructure the CTC to give more in hand to employee.

If an employee whose CTC is higher and falls in tax range then HR should prepare a tax friendly structure to give maximum in hand at the end of financial year based on Tax planner data provided by the employee.

Did I work it right?

May I know the base working? As per the CTC structure, do I get this on hand? [Have a scribbling pad to work out. This is to show that you don't accept whatever they say.] The HR guy will immediately say, 'No, we calculate the other way.' The cat is out. Don't assume the working and later spread a bad mouth that you were betrayed. Check out before you accept the offer. CTC should not be a CTE (cost-to-employee). It could burn your fingers and spoil your mental peace. Ultimately it should not be felt that jumping a job had cost you a size of money. Instead of monetary growth, you should not roll back in ignorance and negligence.

May I have the job description?

This is just to verify the job description discussed with you during the interview. It will give you a clear view of the list of duties you are expected to do. If some of the points were not mentioned to you previously, you can use them to persuade your employer to pay you more. Never assume that the interviewer has fully understood your thought. Asking for JD is the professional way. Seek clarification if need be.

Chapter 18: Begin The Interview

Consider the implications of research findings for your job interviews. Studies indicate that if the interviewer forms a negative impression of the job applicant within the first five minutes of the interview, 90% of the time, the individual is not hired. If the impression is positive during the initial five minutes, 75% of the time, the person will be offered the job.

5.1 Critical Impressions

Impressions formed during the first two to six minutes of the interview are seldom changed during the remaining 30 to 60 minutes of the interview. The maxim "you never get a second chance to make a good first impression" is one worth repeating. Many people still believe the best-qualified person always gets the job. But we act and react to situations based on our perceptions of reality, and thus, our perceptions become our reality.

The same is true with interviewers. The most qualified individual is the one who convinces the interviewer that he or she and no others are the best qualified. As we noted earlier, individuals invited to an interview have already been screened for basic job qualifications. Thus, each interviewee is likely to possess the educational and work experience that is considered necessary for the job. At this point the person who gets the job is the one who impresses the interviewer as being the best for the job. And it is in those critical first few minutes where impressions count the most.

5.2 Win Points with a Positive Image

Appearance is the first thing you communicate with others. Before you have a chance to speak, others notice how you dress and accordingly draw conclusions about your personality and competence. Indeed, research shows that appearance makes the greatest difference when an evaluator has little information about the other person. This is precisely the situation you find yourself in at the start of the interview. In fact, if your appearance is not up to par, you may not even get to the interview. Employment counselors tell us that they meet with many applicants, both for temporary and permanent positions, that dress so inappropriately for a business setting that they cannot even send them on interviews with prospective employers even though their skills would make them viable candidates.

5.3 Overcoming Nervousness

While sitting in the outer office waiting to be called for the interview, you will probably feel nervous. This is normal at a time like this. Instead of trying to rid yourself of these feelings, try to channel them productively. The same physiological process that makes you feel nervous also makes you more alert than normal. It should keep you on your toes and help you respond better to questions during the interview. You can better control your nervousness by following the same advice often given to public speakers. As you walk into the interview room, try to take slow, deep breaths. You can do this subtly so the interviewer will be unaware of it. Although this is easier said than done, the more you can get your mind off yourself and concentrate on the other person, the more comfortable you will feel. If you are nervous, you are probably focusing too much attention on yourself. You are self-consciously concerned with how you are doing and what impression you are making on others. Try to be more other-directed. Rather than concentrate on your needs and fears, concern yourself with the employer's needs and questions.

5.4 Greeting the Interviewer

The receptionist may direct you to meet with the interviewer, or the interviewer may come out to meet you. Either way, stand to your full height before you take a step. Look alert, forceful, and energetic. If the interviewer comes out to meet you, walk over and shake his or her hand firmly. If you are sent to the room where the interviewer is standing, walk toward him or her and shake hands. If he or she is seated and does not look up, stand up, or offer a handshake, you should wait a moment until the interviewer motions for you to be seated. If a lengthy time passes and the interviewer still does not acknowledge you, you may take a seat. However, wait for the interviewer to initiate the conversation.

5.5 Listening

Listening is a learned skill. We learned to listen before we began our formal education, in fact, probably before we can even remember. Hence, we tend to believe listening is something we acquire automatically. While we can probably remember learning to play the piano, play baseball or to type, we usually can't recall learning to listen. Being a good listener takes effort. You can't lean back in your chair and listen passively and listen well. Listening requires active involvement. Good listening will produce several important outcomes.

Give positive nonverbal feedback to the interviewer. Nod in agreement occasionally if you agree and smile occasionally if appropriate. Most everyone likes to receive positive responses from others. Since most people interpret no response as a negative response, avoid an expressionless face. Your feedback is also likely to be interpreted as a sign of interest on your part.

5.6 Employer's Needs

Put yourself in the position of the interviewer for a few moments. You invited a candidate to an interview-based upon his or her cover letter, resume, application form, and perhaps a telephone screening interview. Within a short period of time, a 30 to 60-minute interview, you must now fully assess the interviewee's attitudes, motivations, behaviors, and skills. You want to know what this person can and will do for you. Making a mistake can cost you a great deal of time and money. Studies show companies spend thousands of dollars hiring individuals. The initial costs include announcing the vacancy, screening resumes and letters, interviewing candidates, and settling on a salary/benefit package. The long-term hiring expenses include training costs and the possibility of repeating the whole hiring process which may include unemployment compensation and/or severance pay if the individual must be terminated or resigns. Regardless of how hard you try, you can still make mistakes hiring what appeared to be the best candidate. As many interviewers have learned after years of interviewing experience, assessment techniques are, at best, only rough indicators of performance.

5.7 Use Positive Form

The way you phrase your questions and answers can be as important as the actual content of your communication. What you want to achieve is positive form. This means avoiding negatives by presenting yourself in as positive a light as possible. In the interview, several opportunities arise for enhancing your image through the use of positive form. The first use of positive form relates to names. Each of us likes to be called by our name. Make sure you get the name of the interviewer, get it right, and use it from time to time as you speak. Use the interviewer's title (Miss, Mrs., Mr., Dr., Professor, etc.) and last name. Never call the interviewer by his or her first name unless specifically requested to do so even if the interviewer uses your first name. Many interviewers will be offended by such familiarity.

5.8 Maxims for Effective Interviewing

The following set of generalizations are based upon various topics discussed in the first chapters. These constitute a handy checklist of "do's" and "don'ts" you may want to review just prior to your job interview. Each subject is dealt with more fully in the preceding chapters and can be easily accessed by referring to the Table of Contents.

Interviewing is a communication skill you can successfully learn and apply.

How well your interview will influence your present and future salaries as well as your future relationship with the employer.

You will conduct several job interviews throughout your work life because you will probably change jobs and careers several times.

Successful job interview outcomes include both job offer and rejections.

Effective job interviews take place after conducting several other job search steps identifying skills, stating a job objective, writing resumes and letters, conducting job research, and networking.

Chapter 19: Finding Jobs And Networking

Unless your career goals include a paper hat, the days of simply reading classified ads in the newspaper and perusing job boards to find positions are most likely over. Jobvite's 2013 Social Recruiting Survey found that of the companies surveyed, 73 percent planned to increase their investments in job recruiting via social networking while only 39 percent planned for an increase via job boards. This does not mean job boards cannot be useful; rather, job seekers who aren't using networking and social media are missing out on a substantial portion of job opportunities. To bolster your chances of finding a job that will meet your goals, you should follow both avenues, learning as much as possible about each to stay on top of trends and strengthen your professional interactions.

Job Boards

Job boards are websites where employers list available jobs. Some, such as Craigslist, are general — employer's post jobs across a wide variety of industries. Others are specific; Krop, for example, is a job board geared toward creative industries. Job search engines are similar to job boards in that you can find jobs on them, but instead of employers posting directly to these websites, the websites aggregate job postings from all over the Web. As with job boards, there are both general and industry-specific job search engines, for example, SimplyHired and WorkInRetail.com, respectively. Both types have benefits, but job seekers might turn to job boards before job search engines since they are closer to the source and are not as likely to contain outdated postings. For a listing of the largest job boards and search engines, see the Resources section.

Once you've identified a job you'd like to apply for, take time to read the post carefully before beginning the application process. Most employers ask candidates to apply in a particular manner. Note their preferences regarding cover letters, whom you should address, and requirements for supporting documents and information. After reading the job post, you might make a list of the information you need to give, the documents you need to send, and the preferred formats. As you prepare your cover letter and tweak your resume, refer to your list, so you do not overlook any details. Online job postings can net companies hundreds of applications and resumes; be thorough, and yours will not be thrown out immediately for not following directions.

Networking

Networking requires thoroughness — and patience. Building relationships takes time, and there's no guarantee that your dream job will come to you in a day or a week. If, however, you take advantage of as many networking activities as you have time for, you'll be increasing your chances of meeting a person who's looking for your skills and experience. No matter which platforms or methods you try, though, approach making connections as a mutually beneficial activity. Networking is not about "using" people. A strong networking relationship, whether it begins on Twitter or at a restaurant, helps both parties meet their goals.

Face-to-Face Networking

With the rise of social media websites, job seekers can be forgiven for overlooking fruitful networking opportunities provided by the people and organizations they interact with every day. From your neighbor to your former college advisor, individuals you've already built relationships with may know of just the job you are seeking. Of course, if you are in the High or Medium Priority categories, you'll want to cast a wider net, hopefully forging new connections in the process. Get started widening your circle by exploring the following ways to network face-to-face; tips for how to approach each group are included, so don't be shy.

Friends, Family Members, and Neighbors

When approaching friends, family members, and neighbors, attempt to remain polite and undemanding — you might feel rushed to find a job, but ultimately, they are doing you a favor. Would you rather help someone who respects your time or someone who insists that their problems are your problems? Show that you take your job hunt seriously by asking individuals for a time to meet, and be sure to let them know what it is regarding. You might say, "I am looking for a new position, and I admire your career. Could you spare some time to talk?" Once you meet, listen to what they have to say and let them know your goal. Project yourself as an organized, serious job seeker, one they would not hesitate to mention to their employers for a position.

Alumni Events

Most universities offer alumni networking events, which you can find out about by signing up for your college's alumni email newsletter or list. Events are not necessarily dry, stuffy dinners; you might attend a barbecue or spend an evening at the theater, for example. When making connections among alumni, don't assume that because someone took the same courses as you they'll automatically want to offer you a job or put in a good word for you. Build friendships before asking for career help and treat your alumnus's relationships with the same respect you would a friend or family member.

Networking Events

Make networking events work for you with two steps: choose the right ones, and then work them like a pro. Join a website dedicated to bringing professionals and like-minded individuals together, such as Eventbrite or Meetup. As you decide which events to attend, consider how much each event costs, not just in terms of money but also time. If the event is geared toward professionals in your industry or you respect the speaker, go, but if the event is too general or related to the industry you have no interest in, perhaps skip it. At the event, speak to different people, pass out your resume and business card when appropriate, and don't feel embarrassed about asking for help or to meet at a later date. Moreover, if you tell someone you are going to call, be sure to do so.

Clubs

You are not going to land your next great job by sitting in the house and watching TV. Get involved with others who share your interests. Join a book club, sewing circle, softball team, or volunteer organization. You may or may not be offered an exciting opportunity, but at the very least, you'll fill the need for meaningful interaction. Hunting for a job can be an isolating experience — think of the time spent online or writing cover letters — and you do not want that isolation to drag down your mood. By socializing with people who love what you love, you'll be refreshed through human contact — and you never know who's going to offer you the position you've been dreaming of.

Business Associates

While there is nothing wrong with networking among your business associates, you'll want to proceed with caution if you are looking for a job while still employed. You do not want your boss to find out you are planning on leaving from one of his or her peers, especially if you've badmouthed the organization you are working for. Focus instead on working to a high standard of quality, helping others, and letting it be known that you are always up for new challenges. When the time comes to ask for help, stay positive and professional.

Online Networking

With social media and online networking outlets at the forefront of many businesses' and recruiters' minds, you'll want to do everything you can to take advantage of your presence on the Web. The key here is selectivity — choose a handful of platforms you'll use to forge connections, and don't worry about the rest. Trying to participate in every single social media outlet available will chew through your time in an unproductive manner. Think of social networking like a steak dinner. Instead of a 20-ounce skirt steak, you might opt for a 12-ounce rib eye; you may have less meat, but the quality makes up for what you lack.

As you read through the following listing of the largest social media outlets and tips on how to work them, keep in mind the main aim of using social networking online: securing face-to-face meetings. Seek out professionals in your area who have links to the industry you are in, whether that is animal husbandry or corporate acquisitions, build ties, and then set up a casual get-together for coffee. Just like networking with family or alumni, you might not hear about the perfect position immediately, but you'll increase your chances of a job landing in your lap with each connection you make.

LinkedIn

LinkedIn is far and away the No. 1 social networking tool for job seekers not only because of its popularity but also because of the tools it offers users. Unfortunately, many people do not use LinkedIn to its fullest extent; they upload their resumes, maybe search for a few jobs, and go no further. To truly mine opportunities from this site, you'll first need to build your profile thoroughly, upload a current photo, and setup your custom URL (linkedin.com/in/yourfullname). Next, start building relationships by exchanging endorsements and participating in groups. You'll find groups for nearly every profession — don't be afraid to jump in and join discussions.

Facebook

The number one edict of using Facebook to network is to remember your audience. If you approach the platform with professionalism in mind, you can quickly grow an extensive network through mutual friends, organizations you are a part of. One off-color remark or drunk pic, though, can undo all of your hard work. As you consider what to post to Facebook, ask yourself whether the information is relevant to your professional image. If, for example, you are cultivating a career as an architect, by all means voice your opinions on architectural news, but perhaps save your views on politics for another forum. A reliable rule of thumb is to treat everything you write on Facebook as if it will be read by your grandmother.

Twitter

New users often find that there's a rhythm to Twitter that takes some getting used to. Because every tweet must be 140 characters or less, brevity is the keyword; make your point concisely and avoid unrelated tangents. To get started, you might seek out the biggest names in your profession and follow them, jumping into discussions whenever you have something relevant to add. If you are using both Twitter and Facebook, diversify what you post and whom you talk to on each so that readers have a reason to follow you on both. You'll also have a greater chance of meeting a wider variety of people by expanding each network in a different direction.

MyWorkster

Grads who are fresh out of college can consider joining MyWorkster, a social networking site designed to help college graduates in all types of industries find the companies that are looking for their skills. As with using LinkedIn, be sure to go further than simply uploading your resume. Start discussions, follow and respond to those in your industry, and keep your profile up-to-date.

Google Plus

While Google Plus has not quite reached the popularity of Facebook, enough users prefer it to make it worth your while to investigate. As with Facebook and Twitter, users can add hashtags to posts so that other users who are interested in the same topics will see them. You can also follow other users, just like Twitter and Facebook, which lets you see what they are posting so you can chime in. If you are using Google Plus for professional networking, follow the same rule as for Facebook — only post something if it would not make your grandmother blush.

Industry-Specific Sites

Along with using social networking sites geared toward a general audience, you may wish to consider joining one or two that target individuals in your field. If, for example, you work in the legal profession, you could join lawyrs.net, a LinkedIn-like site for — that is right — lawyers. Because of the popularity of these sites, you should be able to find a social networking site devoted to your industry, no matter what it is.

As you begin to use social media with the goal of making professional connections (as opposed to chatting with old schoolmates), remember that as with networking and finding jobs in general, you are going to need patience. You may also have to change your tactics occasionally, since social media sites fall in and out of popularity faster than reality TV stars. Keep the words of Zig Ziglar in mind, and you'll do fine: "You can have everything in life you want if you will just help other people get what they want." Moreover, if the perfect job still hasn't presented itself, you have one other option: staffing companies.

Chapter 20: Most Common Interview Mistakes

I will list common interview mistakes that mostly happened in the job interview, know them and avoid them.

1. Dressing Inappropriately

When you interview a job, it's imperative to look professional and polished. Despite the fact that your clothing may differ in view of the position you're seeking - for instance, you ought to wear business easygoing garments to a meeting for a non-expert occupation or start up easygoing attire to a meeting at a little new business - its critical look sharp looking and set up together, regardless of what the organization.

2. Arriving Late

Everyone knows that first impressions are very important in landing a job, but did you know that you can make a bad first impression before you even arrive at your interview? Running late proposes poor time administration aptitudes, as well as demonstrates an absence of admiration for the organization, the position and even your questioner.

Go the additional length to verify that you aren't late, and touch base on time, or even early.

3. Bringing a Drink with you

Ditch the coffee or soda before you enter your interview. If you need to fuel up, do it before you get to the interview. Not only is it unprofessional to enter with a drink in hand, but during your interview, you should be focused on the task at hand: making a decent impression, noting inquiries, keeping up eye contact with your potential head honcho, and focusing all through the whole talking procedure.

Having a beverage before you makes the open door for diversion - fiddling with the container, or missing an inquiry while taking a taste, for instance. Also, despite the fact that it might be a moderately improbable plausibility, bringing a beverage into your meeting additionally offers approach to other unattractive mishaps - like spilling the beverage on the work area, on you, or even your questioner!

4. Silence Your Phone during the Interview

Before you get to your interview, silence your phone. Texting during your interview is not only rude and disruptive, as well as it's a really a clear message to your potential head honcho that working for the position you are applying for is not your top priority.

For the same reasons, neither answer calls nor make calls amidst the meeting. To oppose the allurement to check your telephone, stow your telephone in your pack before the meeting.

5. Knowing About the Company

Try not to let your potential executive stump you with the inquiry, "What do you think about this present company?" It's one of the most straightforward inquiries to expert, if you do some examination before your meeting.

Foundation data including organization history, areas, divisions, and a statement of purpose are accessible in an "About Us" segment on most organization sites. Audit it early, then print it out and read it over just before your meeting to revive your memory.

6. Resume Facts

Regardless of the fact that you have presented a resume when you sought the occupation, you might likewise be requested that round out a vocation application. Verify you know the data you will need to finish an application including dates of earlier livelihood, graduation dates, and manager contact data.

It's understandable that some of your older experiences may be hard to recall. Review the facts before your interview.

It can be useful to keep a duplicate of your resume for yourself to allude to amid your meeting, albeit unquestionably don't utilize it as a prop.

Obviously, you ought to never "fudge" any certainties on your resume. The more honest you are on your resume, the better you will have the capacity to examine your past experience amid your meeting.

It's anything but difficult to get diverted amid a meeting; yet not focusing can cost you.

7. Not Paying Attention

Try not to let yourself daydream amid a meeting. Verify you are very much refreshed, ready and arranged for your meeting.

Getting occupied and missing an inquiry looks awful on your part. On the off chance that you daydream, your potential manager will consider how you will have the capacity to stay cantered amid a day at work, on the off chance that you can't even center amid one meeting.

In the event that you feel your consideration disappearing, try to stay locked in.

Keep up eye contact, incline forward marginally when conversing with your questioner, and try to listen adequately.

While you may have no issue focusing in a one-on-one meeting in a private office, it's harder to stay tuned in to the questioner when you're meeting in an open spot. Read all the more about tips for talking in an open spot.

8. Talking too Much

There is not a lot more regrettable than meeting somebody who continues forever and on... The questioner truly doesn't have to know your entire biography. Keep your answers concise, to-the-point and centered and don't meander - just answer the inquiry.

Try not to get diverted begin discussing your own life - your mate, your home life or your youngsters are not themes you ought to dig into. Regardless of how warm, inviting or cheerful your questioner may be, a meeting is an expert circumstance - not an individual one.

Keep away from this misstep by utilizing nonverbal correspondence to awe your potential executive. Additionally look at the main 10 things not to say amid a prospective employee meet-up.

9. Not Being Prepared to Answer Questions

Your interviewer is probably going to ask you more than just the basics about where you worked, and when. To get a vibe of your bent for work, your questioner is going to exploit the dispensed time and tissue out all that he or she needs to think about you as a worker.

Don't let yourself be caught off guard. Prepare for your interview by reviewing what questions to expect, and how to answer them.

Be prepared with a list of questions to ask the employer so you're ready when you asked if you have questions for the interviewer. Examine, well, at the inquiries you ought not to ask amid a prospective employee meet-up and here are the most exceedingly bad meeting answers that you ought to stay away from no matter what.

10. Badmouthing the Past Employers

Don't make the mistake of badmouthing your boss or co-workers. It's sometimes a smaller world than you think and you don't know who your interviewer might know, including that boss who is an idiot... You also don't want the interviewer to think that you might speak that way about his or her company if you leave on terms that aren't the best.

When interviewing for a job, you want your employer to know that you can work well with other people and handle conflicts in a mature and effective way, rather than badmouthing your co-workers or talking about other people's incompetence.

When you're asked hard inquiries, as "Let me know around a period that you didn't function admirably with an administrator. What was the result and how might you have changed the result?" or "Have you worked with somebody you didn't care for? Assuming this is the case, how could you have been able to you handles it?" don't fall back on insulting other individuals. Rather, survey how to answer troublesome inquiries.

Look over more inquiries and replies before your meeting.

11. How to Get a Second Chance with an Employer

Some openings for work can't be spared, yet relying upon the circumstances; you may have the capacity to persuade the head honcho to re-evaluate you. Not all managers have room schedule-wise or assets for a "do-over," however you may be fortunate and discover one who does comprehend that stuff happens and everybody can have a terrible day.

In the event that you think you failed a meeting, take the time to shoot your questioner an email clarifying your circumstances and expressing gratitude toward them for the chance to meeting.

This is what to make on the off chance that you've blown a showing meeting, including a specimen email message to send, in the event that you need to attempt to get another opportunity with the superintendent.

Chapter 21: Writing A Great Resume

A description or review is a text used and created by an individual to show his or her history, abilities and accomplishments. Resumés can be used for a variety of reasons, but most often they are used to secure new jobs. A standard overview provides a "description" of the relevant work experience and training.

Until you start writing or editing your resume, study resume examples that suit a range of job conditions. Then choose a theme and design that better reflects your talents and accomplishments.

Resume Samples A-Z

Use a template The use of a resume template as a starting point allows for personal customization on a pre-designed platform. Attach the details to the resume model, and then change it to show your skills and abilities. How to use resume template resume templates Microsoft word templates for resumes and letters choose best resume format several basic types of resumes are best suited for job openings.

Choose a linear, operational, mix, or tailored resume, depending on your personal and professional circumstances. Decide on one that best suits your work experience, educational background, and skill set. Take the time to customize your resume; it's worth the effort as it doesn't seem to be copied.

Types of Resumes Choose a Simple Font

While preparing your resume, use a simple, easy-to-read font for both hiring managers and candidate management systems. Google is also preferring the simple over the complicated. Most fonts allow your resume simple and easy to read while retaining your individual style.

Resume Font size and Type How Long Should a Resume Be Done?

Add Numbers that Quantify Accomplishments Adding numbers to your resume shows employers in black and white what you've done at work. Not all of the successes is quantifiable, so including those that can act as effective bargaining resources when the question of compensation occurs.

Include Contact Information, With Caveat Include all your contact information so that employers can get in touch with you easily. Please give your full name, street address, city, state, zip code, phone number, and email address. If you have a LinkedIn account or a career blog, please include these references as well. You may not want to provide the full mailing address under certain conditions, but it is generally good enough to do so.

What to Include in the Resume Communication section Create a profile Try using a resume outline or description, with or without a caption, if you want to include a goal in your resume. Remember to tailor your profile to match the job you want to do. The more specific you are, the better your chance of being considered for a job.

Put the most important and relevant achievements first Prioritize the content of your resume so that your most important and relevant experiences are identified first. Describe main milestones at the peak of each rank and, if necessary, measure them.

How to Prioritize The Resume Content Provide Commonly Parsed Keywords

Your resume will include the same keywords as exist in the job descriptions. This way, you increase the chances of your application meeting available positions and being picked for an interview. Sometimes, use keywords in your cover letter, because that message will also be checked. Keywords change with the times, but keep up to date in your business.

Best Techniques to Include on Your Resume How to Provide Keywords in Your Resume Optimize Resume Job

Descriptions Such resume strategies can help you make your details sound impressive, catching the attention of the hiring manager.

Using subtle color highlights to look at important details or quantified achievements. Mix your own theme with the vocabulary that the computer bots can recognize. Good hiring managers will read the same, if possible, under two pages. Bots and humans prefer shorter, more concise resumes Slip Past Software Bots Some tips get you further than others. Resumes These days are often viewed by a robot before a person can see them. This quick and easy-to-use suggestions will help you get your resume through the screening processes. A few simple tweaks can make a difference between getting deleted or reading.

Analysis websites in your field are most likely to be designed for code crawling. Recent examples of upper management will also have been streamlined and are a good overall tool for designing your own resume.

Write a Custom Summary for Every Job Writing a Custom Summary for every job takes more effort, but effort will pay off handsomely, particularly when applying for jobs that suit your skills and experience beautifully. The extra time expended is often returned in the form of interviews.

Review Examples of Each Part of the Summary How to Write a One-Page Summary Targeted Summary Writing and Samples Track Your Work So Summary Updates Are Easy to Send Summaries Properly and With Fixed Attachments When sending an Email Summary, follow the employer's instructions on how to submit your CV. The employer may want your resume to be attached to an email message and sent in a specific format, usually as a Word document or a PDF document. Just do what the employer says.

Chapter 22: What Role Do You Take In Group Projects?

This question is especially popular among hiring managers interviewing college students and recent graduates (good for us). Leadership and initiative are essential components for the success of any person or company, that's exactly what this question will cover.

What the Interviewer is looking for

As mentioned previously, functioning effectively in a team environment is important in nearly any company. In this question, the interviewer is looking to see how you function in a group role and if you are the person who's going to take the initiative and get things done or if you are more of a laid back and go-with-the-flow type of person. In a nutshell, the interviewer wants to know if you are a leader or a follower.

How to NOT Answer this Question

You don't want to answer by showing that you take the leadership role on every project you are assigned to. This is the habit of a bossy, controlling individual. On the other hand, you also don't want to say that you take the backseat in every group project. This shows a lack of initiative, and that you are not willing to take responsibility.

How to Answer this Question

When answering this question, you must first think of a time when you were a part of a group project, especially one in which there were many members involved. Think about the role you took in that project. How did you help the group achieve results? What was your role? How was your role significant to the success of the group? When answering this question, it is important to show the interviewer that you are more than willing to take the initiative in a group assignment. But you also know when to take the backseat and play a significant role in the group's success. You must demonstrate that you know when to lead and you know when to follow.

Sample Answer

Q. What role do you take in group projects?

A. Great question. My role depends solely on the team and the task. For example, one of my weaknesses is Biology. If my team was assigned a task that was Biology-based, I would not take a leadership role because I know that this would not benefit the team. Instead, I would assess everyone's talents and skills. Ideally, the group member who has the most experience in the field will be the project leader because they can more capably delegate tasks. As a team member, it is important to understand that the benefit and success of the team comes first. You must also know when to step up and when to take the backseat but still be able to play the most effective role possible.

This is a fairly generic example. Ideally, you will want to provide an example in which you were part of a group project in which a situation like this has occurred. This answer states that even though you were not the team leader, you still took the initiative to get the team together and assess everyone's talents in order to ensure that the team would develop a successful project. This answer also shows that you know when to step up and be the leader and when to take the backseat. Showing that you are more concerned with the team accomplishment rather than being a leader in every single role shows a lot about your character.

Chapter 23: Questions And Answers: The Top 50 Toughest Questions

A lot of applicants think that mastering a set script for every question in the book is the way to go. This is most certainly not the case. Memorizing a script will make you sound unnatural and insincere. Your interviewer will notice that right away and might try changing or rewording the questions they ask you to throw you off.

Take a look at these best-sellers and learn the core information that the interviewer wants to elicit from these questions. When you know what they're looking for in an answer, impressing them is a breeze.

Tell me something about yourself

This classic question will probably be the first thing that they ask you. Most people make the mistake of talking about what's in their CV's. Don't be one of them. Instead, talk about a hobby of yours or a skill that you have that you think might jive well with the nature of the job (if you did your homework). State examples and experiences of yourself doing this hobby. Show them that you are more interesting that the stuff that's on paper.

Why should I hire you?

They want to see you sell yourself to them. Do not be afraid to highlight your best achievements and tell them how you intend to make better contributions to their company. Here is where you show them that you are a perfect match for the company.

"You should hire me because I have been operating cranes for over five years as of today. I know my way around various models and am well-versed in new trends and technologies when it comes to cranes. I am sure my experience will serve as an asset to your business."

Why should I not hire you?

This trick question comes out when you're doing well and the interviewer believes that you can work your way out of this one. Try a creative answer by telling them you're overqualified and that you will probably get promoted as soon as possible. A little confidence and humor will go a long way here.

Why are you interested in this position?

This is another test of how well you're aware of the job requirements. Go back to your homework and illustrate to your interviewer how your skills and talents will go well with the job. You can also tell them it's your passion and your destined career choice.

"I understand that this job requires a heavy amount of knowledge about stocks and exchange rates. I have been dabbling in the stock market for so long and it has happily rewarded me in terms of financial gains and experience. I believe that experience will deliver plenty of success to your firm."

What do you have to offer our company?

Use your knowledge of the company to your advantage here. Tell them that you are aware of their Mission/Vision statement and show them how your skill sets and attitudes will help them achieve their company goals.

"I understand that your company aims to be the top provider within the country. Having worked for the competition, I am in a great position to help you stand out from the competition to leave your mark onto your clientele."

Where do you see yourself five years from now?

This question wants to see if you have ambitions and goals that involve the company. Do not be afraid to tell them that you intend to be someone of great importance to the company when the time comes. Tell them that you intend to get promoted and handle bigger responsibilities in the future.

Where do you see yourself ten years from now?

This one is a longer version of the earlier question and it asks to see if you have long-term goals. Stick to the earlier answer and tell them that they are involved in your long-term plans.

How do you handle stress?

Don't just show them that you're good with pressure. Explain your step-by-step process about how you handle your time when things start to pile up. Show them that you have an organized personal schematic that helps you perform well even when things go sour.

How do you plan out your day?

Like the earlier question, this one is meant to show them if you're an organized person. Again, talk to them about the specific steps you take after that first cup of coffee in the morning. If they can see that you can plan out your day, they'll know you're self-motivated.

How do you handle conflict?

Besides talking about specific steps, be sure to mention how you will consider the position of the other party before making any personal judgments. Explain how you will consider all sides and options and will try to remain as professional as possible despite have misunderstandings and conflicts with fellow colleagues.

Conclusion

Thank you again for downloading this book!

I hope this book was able to help you to ace any job interview that you are invited to attend. Hopefully, this book will also be instrumental for you to get your dream job.

The next step is to practice these and attend as many interviews as you can!

Thank you and good luck!

www.ingramcontent.com/pod-product-compliance
Lightning Source LLC
Chambersburg PA
CBHW072007070526
44583CB00015B/1377